CONFORMED
to HIS IMAGE
STUDY GUIDE

CONFORMED *to* HIS IMAGE STUDY GUIDE

BIBLICAL, PRACTICAL APPROACHES TO
SPIRITUAL FORMATION

KENNETH BOA, MICHAEL
STEWART, JENNY ABEL

ZONDERVAN ACADEMIC

ZONDERVAN ACADEMIC

Conformed to His Image Study Guide
Copyright © 2020 by Kenneth Boa

Requests for information should be addressed to:
Zondervan, *3900 Sparks Dr. SE, Grand Rapids, Michigan 49546*

Zondervan titles may be purchased in bulk for educational, business, fundraising, or sales promotional use. For information, please email SpecialMarkets@Zondervan.com.

ISBN 978-0-310-10991-4 (softcover)

ISBN 978-0-310-10992-1 (ebook)

Published in association with the literary agency of Wolgemuth & Associates, Inc.

Cover Design: Tammy Johnson
Cover photos: (c) Viktor Gladkov / Shutterstock
Interior Design: Kait Lamphere

Printed in the United States of America

20 21 22 23 24 25 26 27 28 29 30 31 32 /LSC/ 17 16 15 14 13 12 11 10 9 8 7 6 5 4 3 2 1

CONTENTS

HOW TO USE THIS STUDY GUIDE

We rejoice that *Conformed to His Image* has been a trusted resource both in classroom settings and in the lives of individual believers who pursue their call to become more like their Savior. The effectiveness of that resource is in proportion to its scriptural foundation. True spiritual formation is Word-based so that it may result in the complete equipping of those training in righteousness (2 Timothy 3:16–17). We pray that this companion study guide will further that training for those seeking conformity with their utmost calling.

THE GOAL OF THIS STUDY

We hope this study will both broaden and deepen your spiritual understanding while spurring greater commitment to and intimacy with Christ. Our design is not simply to inspire with new insights or applications for each facet (though we desire that to occur). We want these exercises to guide you in Scripture study, which we hope results in the lasting growth and joy found only in observing and meditating on God's Word. Therefore, serious study of the Bible is a major component of this guide. We encourage you not to skip or rush through these exercises but to take your time engaging—and enjoying—the Scriptures. We've created the study so that it can be completed in a year, with a week's break after each of the twelve facets.

Related Materials: This study guide was created in conjunction with a series of forty teaching videos. Although you can benefit from this guide without watching the videos, the videos are referenced periodically and are intended to be watched prior to the completion of each session in the guide.

This study is based extensively, though not entirely, on content in the book *Conformed to His Image, Revised Edition* (Kenneth Boa, Zondervan, 2020). This guide can be completed without this textbook. However, for those who wish to further enrich their understanding of the concepts in each session by following along in the book, we have listed the relevant reading in the book at the start of each session.

For Groups or Individuals: The calling to conform to Christ's image is both individual and corporate, and we created this guide with personal study or group study in mind. All sessions involve individual reflection, which could serve for private growth or for group edification. If you benefit from this guide and its associated resources, please consider forming or leading a group to go through the material.

Introduction

A GEM WITH MANY FACETS

KEY VERSE

Those whom He foreknew, He also predestined to become conformed to the image of His Son, so that He would be the firstborn among many brethren.

Romans 8:29

SUGGESTED READING

Conformed to His Image, Revised Edition, preface and introduction

---

A PILGRIMAGE

The Scriptures speak of our lives as a pilgrimage—we're aliens and strangers in a land that is not our final home. Everyone's on a life journey. The wise will stop to consider where they've been, where they are, and where they're going. They'll also take into consideration the advice and maps of experienced travelers.

Reflect on your journey.

- When and how did you come to faith?

- How would you describe where you are now in your spiritual journey?

Romans 8:29 tells us the purpose of this pilgrimage, and it inspired the title of this study. Read it now and memorize it over the coming days.

> Those whom He foreknew, He also predestined to become *conformed to the image of His Son*, so that He would be the firstborn among many brethren.
>
> Romans 8:29, emphasis added

Growing in Christlikeness begins with forgiveness and new birth in Christ and continues into a lifelong journey of faith and obedience.

➤ This journey is one *with Christ* rather than one *to Christ*. What is the significance of that difference?

Our prayer is that this study causes you to become more desirous of knowing Jesus and growing more into his image.

PRAY: Pray now that your intimacy with Christ would indeed grow and that you would be open to the things God wants to show you in and through this study.

BIBLICAL SPIRITUALITY

This study is organized according to twelve facets of spirituality, each of which is one component in our journey of growth in Christlikeness. You might call these components the sides of a many-faceted gem.

➤ When you hear the term "spirituality" or "spiritual formation," what first enters your mind? (What do you associate these terms with?)

There is no dearth of interest, writings, and teachings on spirituality. In this study, spirituality has a specific definition tethered to the Bible:

> **BIBLICAL SPIRITUALITY:** a Christ-centered orientation to every component of life through the mediating power of the indwelling Holy Spirit

In addition, we will speak of "the spiritual life" often, by which we mean the following:

> **THE SPIRITUAL LIFE:** an all-encompassing, lifelong response to God's gracious initiatives in the lives of people whose trust is centered on the person and work of Jesus Christ

Many other authors have touched on biblical spirituality and the spiritual life.

- What authors in this area have had the greatest impact on you?

- What aspects of or approaches to spirituality did these authors emphasize? (If you're unsure how to answer this, see the list of twelve facets of spirituality on page 5.)

- Do you have specific questions about the spiritual life that you hope to have answered through this study? If so, write them down here.

THE TWELVE FACETS

In this study, you'll be exposed to a variety of approaches to, or facets of, biblical spirituality. Some are associated with more recent movements, others more rooted in historical traditions, and still others more focused on practical application. While they may differ, and some may have been taken to erroneous extremes, these facets reinforce each other and can be integrated into your life. Most important, the written Word of God as well as Christ, the Living Word, are at the center of them all.

Review the list of the twelve facets and their descriptions.

- Which facet(s) do you gravitate toward?

- Which facet(s) do you want to know more about?

> The biblical vision of the spiritual life as a redemptive relationship with the living and personal Creator of all things can satisfy [our] deep desire [for authentic spirituality], but most accounts of this vision are fragmentary or one-sided. The purpose of Conformed to His Image *is to offer a more comprehensive, balanced, and applicable approach to what it means to know Christ. . . . I created these [facets] in an attempt to reflect the various dimensions of biblical truth as they relate to practical experience on a personal and corporate level.*
>
> Conformed to His Image, Revised Edition, 4

THE TWELVE FACETS

Relational Spirituality—Loving God completely, ourselves correctly, and others compassionately

Paradigm Spirituality—Cultivating an eternal rather than a temporal perspective (paradigm) of our lives

Disciplined Spirituality—Engaging in the time-tested, historical disciplines of the spiritual life, such as Bible study, prayer, and solitude

Exchanged Life Spirituality—Identifying with Christ, who gave his life for us so that he might live his life in us

Motivated Spirituality—Seeking to satisfy our innate needs for security, significance, and fulfillment in Christ rather than in the world

Devotional Spirituality—Nourishing intimacy with God by growing to enjoy and trust him more

Holistic Spirituality—Spurning a sacred-secular dichotomy and coming to see every area of life as under the lordship of Christ

Process Spirituality—Growing in Christlikeness through an inside-out rather than an outside-in process

Spirit-Filled Spirituality—Walking in the power of the Holy Spirit, who indwells every believer

Warfare Spirituality—Engaging in the three fronts of spiritual warfare: against the world, the flesh, and the devil

Nurturing Spirituality—Participating with God as he reproduces the life of Christ in others, through a lifestyle of evangelism and discipleship

Corporate Spirituality—Growing in community (not just individually) through encouragement, accountability, and worship

Relational Spirituality

LOVING GOD COMPLETELY

KEY VERSE

You shall love the Lord your God with all your heart, and with all your soul, and with all your mind, and with all your strength.

Mark 12:30

SUGGESTED READING

Conformed to His Image, Revised Edition, chapter 1

AN INSIDE-OUT PROCESS

Loving God is an inside-out process. Yet it's easy to focus on the visible, external actions and choices without considering the invisible, internal aspirations and longings that set us on our course in our relationship with God.

➤ Consider your current aspirations. Could they be characterized as loving God completely? If not, how might you modify those aspirations?

PRAY: We encourage you to approach this guide prayerfully and therefore offer guided prayer in several places. As a way to orient your heart toward loving God, pray as follows:

- Psalm 37:4 says, "Delight yourself in the LORD; and He will give you the desires of your heart." Pray that the desires of your heart may be characterized by a love for the Lord.
- Ask God to purify and inspire your imagination so that you may reflect his image through what you believe, think, say, and do.

God's triunity of being is the foundation and basis for relationships. In God we see the love of the lover (Father), the love of the beloved (Jesus Christ), and the shared love flowing among persons (Holy Spirit).

In what ways does this understanding of the Trinity affect the following?

- Your worship

- Your interaction with others

- Your understanding of how you function in the body of Christ

➢ How does each of these relational elements—worship, interaction with others, and your role in the body of Christ—contribute to life's meaning and richness?

IDENTITY

The more we allow God to define us, the more secure, significant, and satisfied we are. Consider your identity as one both made in the image of God and remade in the image of Christ. How does this identity inform the three key areas of security, significance, and satisfaction? Think of these areas in terms of both the temporal and the eternal.

IMPLICATIONS OF OUR IDENTITY IN CHRIST

	Temporally	Eternally
Security		
Significance		
Satisfaction		

Table 1

Dignity and Depravity

> *Human nature is a web of contradictions. We are at once the grandeur and degradation of the created order; we bear the image of God, but we are ensnared in trespasses and sins. We are capable of harnessing the forces of nature but unable to rule our tongue; we are the most wonderful and creative beings on this planet but the most violent, cruel, and contemptible of earth's inhabitants.*
>
> *Conformed to His Image, Revised Edition,* 12

➤ What false extremes might we fall for if we don't understand that human nature is both dignified and depraved?

➤ How does your understanding of human nature affect your view of yourself? How does it affect your treatment of others?

The Book of Nature

Romans 1:20 declares, "Since the creation of the world His invisible attributes, His eternal power and divine nature, have been clearly seen, being understood through what has been made, so that [people] are without excuse."

➤ Consider the foregoing verse. In what ways does the "book of nature" (a term that refers to God's general revelation to all people through creation) teach us about both God and ourselves?

EXERCISE: Schedule a time this week to immerse yourself in nature. Whether it involves lying under the night sky, walking through a garden, or carefully observing a leaf or anthill, pausing to consider God and his creation—and your role in it—is an act of worship that will bring you closer to God and cultivate gratitude and wonder.

- Time and place I'll spend in worship of my Creator:

DAY BY DAY

Thanks be to thee, O Lord Jesus Christ, for all the benefits which thou hast given us; for all the pains and insults which thou hast borne for us. O most merciful Redeemer, Friend, and Brother, may we *know thee more clearly*, *love thee more dearly*, and *follow thee more nearly*; for thine own sake.

Richard of Chichester (1197–1253), emphases added

Know Thee More Clearly

➤ What is the difference between rational knowledge (knowing via gathering facts or the power of reason) and experiential knowledge (knowing via the senses, relationships, or participation)? Why are both important?

➤ What does Paul's prayer in Ephesians 1:17–18 teach us about the ways in which we may know God more clearly?

> . . . that the God of our Lord Jesus Christ, the Father of glory, may give to you a spirit of wisdom and of revelation in the knowledge of Him . . . that the eyes of your heart may be enlightened, so that you will know what is the hope of His calling, what are the riches of the glory of His inheritance in the saints . . .
>
> Ephesians 1:17-18

The keys to knowing God more clearly are (1) time, (2) communication, and (3) responsiveness to his loving overtures.

➤ Do you desire to know God more clearly?

PRAY: If not, *desiring to desire* him is a good starting point. Pray that God would grant you this desire.

➤ In which of the three key areas (time, communication, and responsiveness) will you commit to pursue knowing God better?

Love Thee More Dearly

The dearness with which we love God is proportional to our understanding of who he is.

➢ Consider this statement about God's Son: *Jesus is not merely the end of a deductive process but a person to be known and loved for himself.* Does this statement correspond with your vision and understanding of God? Why or why not?

➢ Since God is a relational being, how might you better exhibit your love for God by growing deeper in your relationship with others?

Note: Loving God more dearly will be discussed further in the sessions on devotional spirituality.

Follow Thee More Nearly

Following God more nearly requires three great tasks:

1. Willing to do his will
2. Loving the things he loves
3. Choosing the things he sets before us

PRAY: Pray through these three tasks, asking God for "wisdom and . . . revelation in the knowledge of Him" and for the empowerment and enjoyment of loving him completely.

Note: Following God more nearly will be discussed further in the sessions related to holistic and process spirituality.

Relational Spirituality

LOVING OURSELVES CORRECTLY

KEY VERSE

As many as received Him, to them He gave the right to become children of God, even to those who believe in His name.

John 1:12

SUGGESTED READING

Conformed to His Image, Revised Edition, chapter 2

THE WORLD VERSUS THE WORD

> *Only when we define ourselves by the truths of the Word rather than the thinking and experiences of the world can we discover our deepest identity.*
>
> *Conformed to His Image, Revised Edition, 20–21*

LOVING YOURSELF CORRECTLY: choosing to believe that what God says about you is true

➤ How does the notion of loving yourself correctly according to biblical truths contrast with what culture might consider loving yourself?

It takes no effort to have the world fill our minds and hearts with its values. Yet choosing renewal is necessary for daily transformation by the Word's eternal values. The world will define us by default, but God's Word will define us by discipline. Seeing yourself correctly requires:

1. Discipline and exposure to the Word
2. Fellowship and community with like-minded believers

➤ In what measurable way(s) will you increase your exposure to the Word this week?

➤ In what measurable way(s) will you seek meaningful fellowship and community with like-minded believers?

➤ Consider Philemon 6, in which Paul prays that "the fellowship of your faith may become effective through the knowledge of every good thing which is in you for Christ's sake." How does this verse increase your understanding of the relationship among community, exposure to God's Word, and loving yourself correctly?

BEING VERSUS DOING

➤ You fabricate a false self when you base your identity on what you do (or what you have). Consider the following list. In which area(s) are you tempted to base your identity?

- Parents
- Peers
- Power
- Performance
- Possessions
- Pop culture

➤ Are there other ways in which you would be tempted to define yourself if you didn't understand who God is, what God has done for you, and who God says you are?

➤ *Doing* (how we act) should flow out of our *being* (who we are in Christ). Are there things you're currently doing that you do more for appearance or recognition or even for a sense of self-righteousness, rather than out of your identity in Christ?

WHO GOD SAYS YOU ARE

The following are biblical affirmations of who God says you are in Christ. For each affirmation:

- Consider the consequences of not understanding and embracing this identity.
- Ask God to give you an awareness of this identity in your effort to love yourself and others.
- Record your thoughts on how this identity statement affects the key areas of security, significance, and satisfaction.

➢ I am a child of God (John 1:12).

➢ I am a branch of the true vine, and a conduit of Christ's life (John 15:1, 5).

➢ I am a friend of Jesus (John 15:15).

➢ I have been justified and redeemed (Romans 3:24).

➢ I am no longer a slave to sin (Romans 6:6).

➢ I will not be condemned by God (Romans 8:1).

➢ I am a fellow heir with Christ (Romans 8:17).

➢ I have been accepted by Christ (Romans 15:7).

➢ I am joined to the Lord and am one spirit with him (1 Corinthians 6:17).

➢ I am a new creature in Christ (2 Corinthians 5:17).

➢ I have become the righteousness of God in Christ (2 Corinthians 5:21).

➢ I have been made one with all who are in Christ Jesus (Galatians 3:28).

➢ I have been set free in Christ (Galatians 5:1).

➢ I have been blessed with every spiritual blessing in the heavenly places (Ephesians 1:3).

➢ I am chosen, holy, and blameless before God (Ephesians 1:4).

➢ I am God's workmanship created to produce good works (Ephesians 2:10).

➢ I have been brought near to God by the blood of Christ (Ephesians 2:13).

➢ I am a member of Christ's body and a partaker of his promise (Ephesians 3:5; 5:30).

➤ I am light in the Lord (Ephesians 5:8).

➤ I am a citizen of heaven (Philippians 3:20).

➤ I have been made complete in Christ (Colossians 2:10).

➤ I have been raised up with Christ (Colossians 3:1).

We've created an inspirational resource that presents these and other Scripture-based identity statements with moving images and sound. We hope you'll visit that resource at *www.kenboa.org/identity* and find it to be an encouraging reminder of your true identity.

We are no longer defined by the pain of our bounded past but are defined by the joy of our unbounded future. We have a new heredity in Christ, and our future is secure because of our new destiny as members of his body.

Conformed to His Image, Revised Edition, 21

Relational Spirituality

LOVING OTHERS COMPASSIONATELY

KEY VERSE

You shall love your neighbor as yourself.

Matthew 22:39

SUGGESTED READING

Conformed to His Image, Revised Edition, chapter 3

A PROCESS

Though your spiritual birth is instantaneous, spiritual formation is a process. With this principle in mind, answer the following questions.

➤ In what ways is *loving God completely* a process?

➤ In what ways is *loving yourself correctly* a process?

➤ In what ways is *loving others compassionately* a process?

➤ How does grasping your true identity in Christ enable you to love others compassionately?

INVESTING IN ETERNITY

The story of the Bible begins with the eternal relationship of the Trinity. The loving God who created us in his image is the same God who took on our image in the incarnation and sacrificed himself to restore us in eternal righteousness. The risk and reward of relationships are high.

Risk

Even with sincere effort and intention on your part, people may misunderstand or disrespect you.

➤ In what way(s) is this true in the life of Christ? (Suggestion: Reflect on Isaiah 53:1–9 in answering this question.)

➤ Have you experienced being misunderstood or disrespected in your relationships? If so, how?

➤ How will your experience of being misunderstood or disrespected affect your relationships moving forward?

Reward

Even though we undertake great risks in relationships, the rewards of investing our lives in people exceed the pain they can cause.

➤ How does the life of Christ demonstrate the rewards of relationships? (Suggestion: Reflect on Isaiah 53:10–12 in answering this question.)

➤ Have you experienced the rewards of relationships in your own life? If so, how?

➤ How will you remind yourself of the worthiness of pursuing difficult relationships in the face of current pain?

Role Reversal

Loving others compassionately is inextricably linked to loving yourself correctly. While it is exciting and comforting to realize your true identity, it may be less thrilling and more difficult to imagine the true identity of others. Contemplating our relationship with Christ and eternal reward is motivating, but maturity may be marked by the extent to which we contemplate the identity and eternity of others.

Consider this portion of C. S. Lewis's famous sermon *The Weight of Glory,* mentioned in this video session:

> It may be possible for each to think too much of his own potential glory hereafter; it is hardly possible for him to think too often or too deeply about that of his neighbor. The load, or weight, or burden of my neighbor's glory should be laid daily on my back, a load so heavy that only humility can carry it, and the backs of the proud will be broken. It is a serious thing to live in a society of possible gods and goddesses, to remember that the dullest and most uninteresting person you talk to may one day be a creature which, if you saw it now, you would be strongly tempted to worship, or else a horror and a corruption such as you now meet, if at all, only in a nightmare. All day long we are, in some degree, helping each other to one or other of these destinations. It is in the light of these overwhelming possibilities, it is with the awe and the circumspection proper to them, that we should conduct all our dealings with one another, all friendships, all loves, all play, all politics. *There are no ordinary people. You have never talked to a mere mortal.*
>
> C. S. Lewis, *The Weight of Glory,* emphasis added

➤ How does viewing relationships in light of eternity change your perspective and attitude toward others in the here and now?

FORGIVENESS REQUIRED

Investing in relationships involves forgiveness. But often we do not forgive because, as with so many other sins, our tendency is to focus on ourselves. Assess the following tendencies when it comes to forgiveness.

- Making excuses
- Assigning blame
- Seeking justice

➢ Is there one that traps you? Why might that be?

➢ What is the biblical alternative to each of these tendencies?

IDENTITY AND IMITATION

If we love God, we'll love the people he loves. Christ set an example of how to do this. Most famously, during his last night with the disciples, Jesus served his disciples, despite knowing that one (Judas) would betray him and the others would abandon him in his final hours.

> Before the Feast of the Passover, Jesus knowing that His hour had come that He would depart out of this world to the Father, having loved His own who were in the world, He loved them to the end. During supper, the devil having already put into the heart of Judas Iscariot, the son of Simon, to betray Him, *Jesus, knowing that the Father had given all things into His hands, and that He had come forth from God and was going back to God*, got up from supper, and laid aside His garments; and taking a towel, He girded Himself. Then He poured water into the basin, and began to wash the disciples' feet and to wipe them with the towel with which He was girded.
>
> John 13:1-5, emphasis added

➢ What lessons can we learn from Christ's understanding of his own identity and subsequent choice to serve despite relational difficulties?

➢ Loving others may be demonstrated externally in acts of service, and as we conform to Christ's image, these external acts flow from internal characteristics. Read Philippians 2:1–5. What internal characteristics are key to imitating Christ?

If there is any encouragement in Christ, if there is any consolation of love, if there is any fellowship of the Spirit, if any affection and compassion, make my joy complete by being of the same mind, maintaining the same love, united in spirit, intent on one purpose. Do nothing from selfishness or empty conceit, but with humility of mind regard one another as more important than yourselves; do not merely look out for your own personal interests, but also for the interests of others. Have this attitude in yourselves which was also in Christ Jesus.

Philippians 2:1-5

John 13:3 teaches that Jesus knew the following things about himself:

1. His *dignity* and *power*
2. His *significance* and *identity*
3. His *security* and *destiny*

We're able to imitate Jesus because our identity is in him, and his resources are our resources. As believers, we too can know great truths regarding our dignity, power, significance, identity, security, and destiny. Explore these characteristics found in the following verses. Use the space to record your notes.

- Dignity and power: Ephesians 1:3, 19; 3:16, 20–21

- Significance and identity: Romans 8:16; 1 John 3:1–2

- Security and destiny: Romans 8:18, 35–39

Paradigm Spirituality

LIFE IS A JOURNEY, BUT WHERE ARE WE GOING?

KEY VERSE

Lord, make me to know my end
And what is the extent of my days.

Psalm 39:4

SUGGESTED READING
Conformed to His Image, Revised Edition, chapter 4

THE BREVITY OF LIFE

Fill in the date of your birth in the following blank.

_____ — ????
(Your birthday)   (Date known only to God)

We're all living in the period of the dash, between two dates: your birthday (which you know) and the day you will die (which only God knows).

➢ A good exercise for determining whether you're spending your years well and wisely is to imagine that you have only one year left to live. How would you spend your remaining time? What would you do differently than you're doing now?

➢ Are you willing to live in the way you just described? Why or why not?

The days of the years of our lives are few, and swifter than a weaver's shuttle. Life is a short and fevered rehearsal for a concert we cannot stay to give. Just when we appear to have attained some proficiency, we are forced to lay our instruments down. There is simply not time enough to think, to become, to perform what the constitution of our natures indicates we are capable of.

A. W. Tozer, *Knowledge of the Holy*

➢ How aware are you of your mortality? Do you ever ponder your mortality, or do you tend to feel or live as if you have all the time in the world?

➢ Read Job 7:7–10, a portion of which inspired part of Tozer's quote. Write down any thoughts or reflections on the truth the passage reveals.

➢ Next read Psalm 39:4–7 and Psalm 90. Note any themes in common with the Job passage and Tozer quote.

As for the days of our life, they contain seventy years,

Or if due to strength, eighty years,

Yet their pride is but labor and sorrow;

For soon it is gone and we fly away. . . .

So teach us to number our days,

That we may present to You a heart of wisdom.

Psalm 90:10–12

➤ If our earthly lives are so fleeting, as these verses suggest, why do so many people— even Christians—act as though they'll live forever, as though this world were our permanent home?

If we want to be wise, we will treat things according to their true value: the eternal as eternal, the temporal as temporal.

• Are you valuing anything transitory too highly? (If so, what?)

• Are you valuing anything that has eternal worth too little? (If so, what?)

• What are the things that endure—the things that matter most from an eternal standpoint?

Age conspires with God to take away our temporal hope. Many of us come to realize our mortality in a real sense, rather than only theoretically, around midlife (ages thirty-eight to forty-five), though it can come earlier or later for some. At that point, we realize we aren't going to be able to do all the things we hoped and dreamed we would do. Instead of a crisis, however, this time in our lives can be a process of realizing that even if we accomplish much in this life and succeed in various ways, we will never scratch the surface of our deepest longings, because we were made for eternity. And only the eternal God will fully satisfy those longings.

PRAY: Pray for an awareness of the fleetingness of life. Consider using Psalm 39:4 to pray, "Lord, make me to know my end and what is the extent of my days."

PARADIGM SHIFT

PARADIGM: a way of seeing—a lens through which we envision things

Fill in the two blank blocks at the bottom of table 2. Then ponder your awareness of these competing ways of seeing the world.

THE COMPETING PARADIGMS OF LIFE

	Temporal Paradigm	Eternal (Biblical) Paradigm
Centered on . . .	Self	Christ
Presuppositions	Matter, energy, space, and time are all that's real (naturalism/materialism). OR Life is an illusion—nothing we see is real (Eastern religions).	Our life on earth is a brief pilgrimage preparing us for eternity.
Values and Priorities		

Table 2

➤ Evaluate your life outlook and activities. Are you currently approaching life more with an eternal or temporal paradigm? How do you know?

➤ Could you use a paradigm shift? If so, what should that shift entail?

Most of us find ourselves oscillating between the eternal and temporal value systems. Even if we know we're supposed to be pursuing the eternal, we often don't. There's a human tendency to try to keep one foot in the world and one in God's kingdom. This leads to a divided heart and life, as well as to anxiety and frustration.

➤ Why, in your opinion, do we fluctuate between these two value systems so much?

➤ What do you think of the following quote, which upends the common misconception that people who are heavenly minded are of no earthly good? Have you seen this misconception at work in your life or in the lives of others?

Does this mean that we should be so heavenly minded that we are of no earthly good? In fact, it is the opposite—when people become heavenly minded, they treasure the passing opportunities of this life and become more alive to the present moment. Rather than being overwhelmed with the problems of life, they understand that these too will pass and that "the sufferings of this present time are not worthy to be compared with the glory that is to be revealed to us" (Romans 8:18). Instead of taking things for granted, they learn to savor blessings and joys that are otherwise overlooked.

Conformed to His Image, Revised Edition, 49

LIVING IN LIGHT OF THE END

The destination determines the journey. Wisdom invites us to see that we're heading somewhere; we're not going in circles. We need to prepare for home and not be so focused on the things of this world that we miss out on the things of the next.

➤ Where are *you* headed after life on earth? How do you know?

➤ How much is your final destination affecting your current journey through life?

➤ *So many people are focused on the little details of life—more on the journey than on the destination.* Does this assessment describe you? If so, is there a particular area in which you're overly focused on this world?

To treasure the precious present is to desire that which is going to endure. It means to treat every day for what it really is: preparation for our eternal home in heaven. If we're wise, we'll treat our time as if we have only two days on our calendar—today and *that* day, the day when we'll stand before Jesus.

➤ Read Ephesians 5:15–17. How does embracing the "precious present" help prepare us for eternity?

Be careful how you walk, not as unwise men but as wise, making the most of your time, because the days are evil. So then do not be foolish, but understand what the will of the Lord is.

Ephesians 5:15–17

PRAY: Ask God for the wisdom to pursue that which endures—the things which matter most in the end.

➤ Write down anything you plan to see, think, or do differently in light of your *telos* (end or goal).

Paradigm Spirituality

CAN WE TRUST GOD?

KEY VERSE

Faith is the assurance of things hoped for, the conviction of things not seen.

Hebrews 11:1

SUGGESTED READING

Conformed to His Image, Revised Edition, chapter 5

PRESUPPOSITIONS

> *The only path to . . . true fulfillment lies in consciously choosing God's value system over that which this world offers. This choice is based on trusting a Person we have not yet seen. "And though you have not seen Him, you love Him, and though you do not see Him now, but believe in Him, you greatly rejoice with joy inexpressible and full of glory, obtaining as the outcome of your faith the salvation of your souls" (1 Peter 1:8–9).*
>
> *Conformed to His Image, Revised Edition,* 56

The previous session described two basic ways of seeing the world—with an eternal paradigm or a temporal paradigm. These paradigms represent rival value systems that compete for our allegiance and attention. The values of these two paradigms differ, and therefore so do their outcomes.

Review table 3, and then answer the questions after it.

VALUES AND OUTCOMES OF RIVAL PARADIGMS

Temporal	Eternal
Pleasure	Knowing God
Recognition of people	Approval of God
Popularity	Servanthood
Wealth and status	Integrity and character
Power	Humility
↓	↓
Emptiness	Fulfillment
Delusion	Reality
Foolishness	Wisdom

Table 3

➤ From the table, what temporal pursuit(s) do you find most alluring? (You can get even more specific than the broad categories given in the table.)

➤ Have you experienced the emptiness, delusion, and foolishness which result from engaging in that pursuit? If so, how?

➤ What eternal value(s) can you embrace instead, resulting in fulfillment, an understanding of true reality, and wisdom?

➤ Ecclesiastes 1–6 contains eighteen mentions of an "under the sun" view of life. Scan these chapters for evidence of a temporal paradigm. What similarities do you see with the values listed in the table?

➢ Now read Hebrews 11. In this famous chapter, we see the walk of faith portrayed. The people mentioned in the chapter approached life with an eternal paradigm. What are some of the values they embraced? What was the outcome of their lives?

Prosperity knits a man to the World. He feels that he is "finding his place in it," while really it is finding its place in him. His increasing reputation, his widening circle of acquaintances, his sense of importance, the growing pressure of absorbing and agreeable work, build up in him a sense of being really at home in earth.

C. S. Lewis, *The Screwtape Letters*

PRAY: Ask God to show you how to pursue and implement the values of his kingdom in your life. Write out what he shows you in the space provided. If it's helpful to you, use the following outline of eternal values.

Knowing God
Approval of God
Servanthood
Integrity and character
Humility

PERSPECTIVE

Our presuppositions shape our perspective.

If ours is an eternal perspective, we will be gripped by the biblical truth that our brief earthly sojourn is designed to prepare us for an eternal heavenly citizenship.

Conformed to His Image, Revised Edition, 57–58

➤ How closely does your current perspective match the description in the quote? Are you gripped by this biblical truth that you're a sojourner—a pilgrim or wayfarer just passing through this world to the next?

➤ Revisit the book of Hebrews, looking at verses 11:9–19 and 13:14. How do these verses depict an eternal perspective?

By faith he [Abraham] lived as an alien in the land of promise, as in a foreign land, dwelling in tents with Isaac and Jacob, fellow heirs of the same promise; for he was looking for the city which has foundations, whose architect and builder is God.

Hebrews 11:9–10

Here we do not have a lasting city, but we are seeking the city which is to come.

Hebrews 13:14

PRAY: Ask God to align your perspective with that of these verses. Ask him to help you treasure and pursue that which endures.

> When we travel to another country, we must exchange our currency. The currencies of this world will do us no good in the next unless we previously invested them for Christ's sake in the lives of other people. Others-centered relationships that express the love of Christ are the currency of heaven.
>
> *Conformed to His Image, Revised Edition*, 58

➤ What's one thing you can do to invest the currencies of this world into the lives of others for Christ's sake?

EXERCISE: Moments of intimacy, beauty, and adventure provide us with hints of home. They're pointers to our heavenly destination—what C. S. Lewis described in his *Letters to Malcolm: Chiefly on Prayer* as "'patches of Godlight' in the woods of our experience." These moments can point us to the lasting city to come. Remember these moments in your life. Use the space provided to reflect on how those moments point to your heavenly home.

• Intimacy

• Beauty

• Adventure

By the same token, moments of alienation, ugliness, and boredom (*ennui*) remind us that we are not home yet. Remember a few of these moments as well, as painful as they may be, and consider how they too remind you of your eternal destination.

• Alienation

• Ugliness

• Boredom (*ennui*)

PRIORITIES AND PRACTICE

Our presuppositions shape our perspective, our perspective in turn shapes our priorities, and our priorities shape our practice.

EXERCISE:

➤ First, list the top two or three of your *desired priorities* (based on an eternal perspective):
   1.
   2.
   3.

➤ Next, review your *practices* by looking through (1) your calendar and (2) your bank record from the past month. What do your top *priorities* in life appear to be? List them below.

   • Top priorities based on how I spent my time:
      1.
      2.
      3.

   • Top priorities based on how I spent my money (you may want to consider only discretionary funds, as top spending items are likely essentials such as housing and food):
      1.
      2.
      3.

➤ Finally, compare your lists. Do your desired priorities match up with ones revealed by your use of time and your pocketbook? If not, why not? What adjustments do you need to make?

That which is highly esteemed among men is detestable in the sight of God.

Luke 16:15

➤ Think about the end of your life, when you will meet Jesus face to face. Write your obituary. What are you remembered for? What did you leave behind? What are you taking with you to the ultimate show-and-tell? (This doesn't have to be a morbid exercise. Have fun with it! The point is to get a sense of whether your practice reveals eternal presuppositions, perspective, and priorities. Better to recalibrate now while you still have the opportunity!)

PRAY: Ask God, again, to help you recalibrate your paradigm (the way you see the world) and to fully trust him with your life, including both your time and your material possessions and resources.

What we do in life echoes in eternity.

Maximus, *Gladiator*

Disciplined Spirituality

DEPENDENCE AND DISCIPLINE

KEY VERSES

Work out your salvation with fear and trembling; for it is God who is at work in you, both to will and to work for His good pleasure.

Philippians 2:12–13

SUGGESTED READING
Conformed to His Image, Revised Edition, chapter 6

AVOIDING THE EXTREMES

The spiritual life is both human and divine. . . . On the human side, we are responsible to work out, not work for, our salvation. On the divine side, God gives us the desire and empowerment to accomplish his purposes.

Conformed to His Image, Revised Edition, 64

The process of spiritual growth involves a divine-human synergy: God's work in us *and* our work to abide in and walk with him. Grace is not opposed to effort; it's opposed to earning. Still, we have to guard against overemphasizing the human side of the equation, just as we must avoid emphasizing God's sovereignty so much that we become spiritually passive.

DISCIPLINED SPIRITUALITY: TWO EXTREME APPROACHES

	Extreme 1: Overemphasizes our role, minimizes God's role	Extreme 2: Overemphasizes God's role, minimizes our role
Characterized by	Striving for, living for Jesus without depending on the Spirit's power	Let-go-and-let-God passivity
Emphasizes	Knowledge, rules, rededication efforts, human activities	Experience, the supernatural, the person of the Holy Spirit
Downplays or ignores	The ministry of the Holy Spirit	Human effort and responsibility

Table 4

➤ Examine table 4. In your faith, do you lean toward one of the two extremes? If so, which one?

➤ What is the potential danger in that leaning?

Many passages in Scripture reveal the interrelationship between the human and the divine in the Christian life. Read the following passages, and then write down how each one defines our role versus God's role in our relationship with him.

• John 15:4–11

Human role:

Divine role:

- Galatians 2:20

    Human role:

    Divine role:

- 2 Peter 1:1–11

    Human role:

    Divine role:

If we live by the Spirit, let us also walk by the Spirit.

Galatians 5:25

The word translated as "walk" in Galatians 5:25 refers to conforming with or following a standard. It encourages us to live with a mindset of aligning with the Spirit on a day-by-day basis.

➤ How often do you recognize your need to depend on the Spirit's power in all that you do? Are you aware of this regularly or only occasionally?

PRAY: Pray that you will become more attuned to this need of dependence, realizing that any of your efforts apart from him are futile (John 15:5).

BENEFITS OF DISCIPLINE

Spirituality is not instantaneous or haphazard; it is developed and refined. . . . The spiritual life is progressively cultivated in the disciplines of the faith; you and I will not wake up one morning to find ourselves suddenly spiritual.

Conformed to His Image, Revised Edition, 65

Many Christians lose their initial fire for the Lord and bench themselves, staying on the sidelines instead of in the "game" of growing in Christlikeness.

➤ Honestly assess your life. Have you benched yourself at some point? Are you doing it now?

➤ If so, what will it take to get back in the game?

➤ Wisdom is skill in the art of living. Proverbs 4:7 admonishes us, "Though it cost all you have, get understanding" (NIV). Think of a skill you have, such as the ability to play a particular musical instrument or sport. What amount of discipline and devotion did you put into developing that skill? (What price did you have to pay to gain it?)

➤ What would happen if you stopped practicing for a day? A week? A year?

➤ How is this similar to the spiritual life?

Discipline yourself for the purpose of godliness.

1 Timothy 4:7

I will walk about in freedom, for I have sought out your precepts.

Psalm 119:45 NIV

Too often we see discipline as enslaving, associating it with legalism and tyranny. In reality, discipline leads to freedom, not bondage. It's like the rails that keep us on track, heading in the right direction. This view of discipline has been held and applied by all the great saints of history. However, we need to be properly motivated, or disciplines will drain us instead of invigorate us.

➤ What are some of the benefits to spiritual disciplines?

➤ Which of these motivates you the most?

➤ How does discipline give us options we never would have had otherwise?

The video session mentioned what Dallas Willard calls "the law of indirect preparedness." This refers to "the disciplines in the background of our lives [which] prepare us for the unexpected times when we will need to respond in appropriate ways" (*Conformed to His Image, Revised Edition*, 67).

• Have you ever been caught unprepared spiritually?

• Why is it important to train in discipline regularly, rather than only when you feel you need to?

Discipline may seem unappealing, but if we keep the goal in sight—knowing Christ and becoming more like him—and view discipline as a means to that end, then we can begin to desire it rather than dread it.

➤ What do you want more than anything else in life?

➤ If knowing Christ and becoming more like him isn't currently your primary desire, do you want it to be? If knowing him better isn't your chief desire, what's holding you back from paying the price necessary—in time, resources, and energy—to do the things that will bring you closer to him?

➤ Read Proverbs 2. Write one or two phrases that stick out to you most, and then use them to offer a prayer to God for the will and desire to pursue him and his wisdom above everything else.

We have bought the illusion that we can be like Christ without imitating his spirituality. If we wish to be like our Master, we must imitate his practice. . . . We desire to know Christ more deeply, but we shun the lifestyle that would make it happen.

Conformed to His Image, Revised Edition, 66–67

TRAINING AND PRACTICE

There are no shortcuts to spiritual growth. And it's not a matter of trying harder; it's a matter of training. It's not a matter of more time; it's a matter of intentionality with the time we do have.

➤ What are some points during your daily routines when you can intentionally practice disciplines—principally prayer as well as reading and studying Scripture—that bring you closer to God? Commit to doing at least one of these for a week and see what difference it makes.[1]

You can't get rid of bad, sinful habits by simply extinguishing them (the "extinction method"). Instead, you need to replace them with good habits.

- What's one specific sinful tendency or habit that you need to eliminate from your life?

- Have you tried doing so via the extinction method? How did that go?

- What good practice(s) can you replace that bad habit with?

The goal of spiritual disciplines is to know, love, and trust God more. This happens with time, through consistent practice. (See figure 1.)

DAILY CHOICES ❭ **HABITS** ❭ **CHARACTER** ❭ **DECISIONS**

Figure 1

The key to discipline is to be more focused on inner transformation (formation of character) than on outward routines. Spiritual growth is an inside-out process, not an outside-in one.

➤ Have you tended to regard disciplines of the faith with an outward-in rather than an inside-out mentality? (Do you practice certain disciplines—pray, read the Bible, attend church or Bible study—just to check off a mental box? This is known as externalism.)

➤ How can you remain committed to spiritual practices without falling into the trap of externalism? Brainstorm at least one or two specific ideas.

There is no *shalom* (wholeness, unity of life) without *shabbat* (rest). Coming away from the busyness of everyday life for rest, reflection, and renewal is a critical practice for reestablishing our dependence on God rather than on our own efforts. During this time, we can nourish a vibrant and intimate relationship with him amid a harried life.

➤ Evaluate your current discipline of taking a rest from your work and responsibilities. Do you even do this? How often and when?

➤ It can be easy to allow work to invade rest, especially in today's 24/7 world of connectedness. Do you have a cutoff for when you stop working each day?

➤ What about a cutoff for when you stop scrolling through your phone or other electronic device?

EXERCISE: Try setting one of these cutoffs for a week and see what difference it makes in you.

EXERCISE: Put one or both of the following on your calendar:

1. Ten minutes of daily rest (at minimum)
2. A few hours of weekly rest (doesn't have to be on Sunday)

Use these times to draw near to God in an intentional way. Consider reading a psalm as a prayer or taking a leisurely walk while in conversation with God.

> If anyone wishes to come after Me, he must deny himself, and take up his cross daily and follow Me.
>
> Luke 9:23

Disciplined Spirituality

WHAT ARE THE SPIRITUAL DISCIPLINES?

KEY VERSES

Discipline yourself for the purpose of godliness; for bodily discipline is only of little profit, but godliness is profitable for all things, since it holds promise for the present life and also for the life to come.

1 Timothy 4:7–8

SUGGESTED READING

Conformed to His Image, Revised Edition, chapter 7

AN OVERVIEW OF TWENTY DISCIPLINES

Run in such a way that you may win.

1 Corinthians 9:24

Life is to be lived in a gymnasium, not just a living room. Once we have become new creations in Christ, we have the Holy Spirit in us, empowering and motivating us to train in righteousness, to flex and strengthen our spiritual muscles.

Spiritual disciplines are not ends in themselves or boxes to check off a list but practices that Jesus himself pursued with the purpose of drawing close to his Father. Some are disciplines of abstinence (refraining from something), while others are disciplines of engagement (acting toward something). Many can be pursued corporately as well as individually.

> *It would be a mistake to claim that every follower of Christ should practice all of these disciplines in a consistent or rigorous way. . . . You will be drawn to some and indifferent to others. Still, it is wise to engage occasionally in the ones you would normally dismiss, so that you can experience their unique benefits.*
>
> *Conformed to His Image, Revised Edition, 72*

On the next page is a list of twenty disciplines you can pursue for spiritual gain.[2]

- Read through the list and place a check beside the ones you've engaged in.
- Of these twenty disciplines, which are you *most* drawn to? Place a star beside those.
- Which are you *least* drawn to? Place a dash beside those.
- Finally, pick two disciplines you'll plan to engage in this week, and decide how and when you'll practice them. Try to pick at least one that you're either inexperienced in or less drawn to.

Discipline 1:

How I'll practice it:

When:

Discipline 2:

How I'll practice it:

When:

TWENTY SPIRITUAL DISCIPLINES

1. *Solitude*—moving away for a time from the lures and aspirations of the world, from the influence of peers and society, and into God's presence
2. *Silence*—a catalyst of solitude, involves quieting the noises of our surroundings and/or observing times of restricted speech in the presence of others
3. *Prayer*—personal communion and dialogue with God; not limited to structured times but an ongoing dialogue as we go about our activities
4. *Journaling*—keeping a spiritual diary to record thoughts, feelings, and experiences; helps us understand the process of growth God is taking us through
5. *Study*—not only reading God's Word but actively engaging with it (through observation, interpretation, and application); can also include reflection on nature or the writings of others
6. *Meditation*—focusing the mind on revealed truth (*different* from the Eastern concept, which involves emptying the mind); pondering a verse or passage and letting it sink deeply into us (a close relative of prayer and study, meditation depends on solitude and silence)
7. *Fasting*—abstaining from physical nourishment for the purpose of spiritual sustenance; can also be broadened to include other types of abstention, for the purpose of promoting self-control and revealing the extent to which we're ruled by our appetites
8. *Chastity*—pursuing sexual purity (whether single or married) by resisting improper feelings, fantasies, obsessions, and relations
9. *Secrecy*—choosing anonymity before people so that we seek God's praise and approval alone instead of insisting on getting the credit or recognition we think we deserve
10. *Confession*—appropriately uncovering and revealing to others our sins, weaknesses, and failures, thus setting us free from the burden of hidden sin
11. *Fellowship*—seeking the community of other believers for mutual encouragement and edification; helps us see and appreciate the interconnectedness of the body of Christ (especially important for those of us who grew up in a culture that emphasizes individualism and self-sufficiency)

12. *Submission*—voluntarily submitting to others as an expression of our submission to Christ; a form of self-denial, in which we seek others' good over our rights

13. *Guidance*—seeking spiritual direction through accountability to a mentor whose credibility has been established by experience and maturity; the Holy Spirit is our primary guide and counselor, and we must remember that human guides, however mature, are still fallible

14. *Simplicity*—willingly abstaining from using resources at our disposal for our gratification and aggrandizement (also known as frugality)

15. *Stewardship*—reviewing how we invest the time, talent, treasure, truth, and relationships we've been given, because of our view of ourselves as managers of Another's estate

16. *Sacrifice*—more radical than simplicity, involves the risk of giving up something we would use to meet not just our wants but our needs (and entrusting ourselves to God's care)

17. *Worship*—being fully occupied with the attributes of God: the majesty, beauty, and goodness of his person, powers, and perfections

18. *Celebration*—focusing on and taking pleasure in all that God has done on our behalf; choosing gratitude over grumbling, remembrance over indifference

19. *Service*—showing kindness, courtesy, sensitivity, and concern for people, out of love for Jesus and a desire to follow his example rather than out of a desire for recognition

20. *Witness*—going beyond the circle of our believing friends and investing in relationships with people who have not yet met Christ; evangelism with a corresponding lifestyle

SOLITUDE AND SILENCE

Solitude and silence are two of the disciplines of abstinence (others include fasting, chastity, secrecy, and simplicity). Both practices are fundamental, helping us to become more authentic people who live out of the depths of who we are in Christ rather than according to a false self-image we've created for ourselves.

Throughout his ministry, no matter how busy he was, Jesus found time for solitude. Read the following verses and describe what you observe about Jesus' practice of solitude and silence.

- Matthew 14:23

- Mark 1:35

- Luke 5:16

Jesus often withdrew in solitude before major events, such as the advent of his public ministry (Matthew 4:1–11), the choosing of the twelve disciples (Luke 6:12–16), and his prayer in the garden of Gethsemane before he sacrificed himself on the cross (Matthew 26:36–46).

➤ Is there any upcoming event or major decision for which you need to make a special effort to withdraw to a place of solitude to pray and seek God's presence and guidance?

➤ Having a consistent time and place for solitude (and for prayer and Bible study) are important for making this discipline a habit. Do you have these already, and if so, what are they?

➤ If not, how might you make this discipline a more regular part of your routine? (Suggestion: Start with just ten minutes each day.)

People who are more extroverted may be tempted to avoid the discipline of solitude, while introverts relish the time alone—sometimes too much! There's a danger in either extreme. And even being alone doesn't automatically lead to an honest and open time with God, because we can all put on a mask whether we're by ourselves or with other people.

EXERCISE: Take a moment right now, or later tonight if you're in a group study, for solitude. Spend fifteen minutes simply sitting and enjoying God's presence. Silence all electronics, preferably putting them in another room or out of sight.

EXERCISE: If you're in a busy or stressful season of life right now, consider whether a more extended time away—perhaps a half-day retreat or a few hours one afternoon—would be beneficial. Then take the steps needed to make it happen.

EXERCISE: The next time you pray or read God's Word, first ask God to direct your prayers and thoughts and to set the agenda of your time together; then take five to ten minutes of sitting in "quietness and trust" (Isaiah 30:15) before him. Don't rush into your thoughts and requests.

➤ In addition to practicing *silence before God*, practicing *silence before people* can be a powerful discipline. Be honest with yourself and consider how much you struggle with remaining silent. Do you often feel you say too much? Speak too soon or without thinking? Hurt others by speaking too critically, rudely, or sarcastically?

EXERCISE: If you struggle in this area, plan a verbal fast to help you tame your tongue. You can do one of the following:

- Stay silent for an entire day (inform others of this decision first!).
- For a full day or week, plan to only listen to others, without giving your opinion or advice, unless it's explicitly requested. (If this is a struggle with a particular person, such as a spouse, focus the exercise on him or her.)

> When there are many words, transgression is unavoidable,
> But he who restrains his lips is wise.
>
> Proverbs 10:19

STUDY, MEDITATION, AND PRAYER

The most important disciplines of engagement are study, meditation, and prayer. Jesus did not consider these disciplines optional, so they shouldn't be optional for his followers either. Jesus was a man of deep and regular prayer and a student of God's Word. These practices weren't burdens to him, nor should they be to us; they're the means by which we come to know and love God more.

Study

➢ Read 2 Timothy 3:16–17. What does this passage say about the benefits of studying the Bible?

➢ Assess your current Bible reading and study habit. Do you have a habit at all? If not, do you want to develop one? (If so, see the tips at the bottom of this page.)

➢ How much do you rely on books about the Bible for knowledge of the Bible, versus studying God's Word directly for yourself?

➢ A key but often forgotten step in Bible study is seeking to apply what you read. How well do you do with this step? How can you be more intentional in application?

TIPS FOR BIBLE STUDY

- Find a consistent time and place for study.
- Invite God into your time in the Word, asking him to open your eyes to his truth.
- Approach the Bible not merely as a textbook but as the living and active Word of God.
- Purpose ahead of time to obey and apply what you read.
- If you get into a rut, change your routine. Seek "fresh bread" each time you study.
- Have a plan! One option: Grab four bookmarks. Place one each at Genesis 1, Psalm 1, Matthew 1, and Acts 1. Every day, read a portion from each section (however much you'd like), leaving your bookmarks where you stop. Try to stick with this pattern until you've read through the entire Bible. This plan gives a balanced diet of the full counsel of Scripture.

Meditation

> I will meditate on Your precepts
> And regard Your ways.

Psalm 119:15

Christian meditation is about dwelling—setting your mind—on what is true, honorable, right, pure, lovely, of good repute, excellent, and praiseworthy (Philippians 4:8). It is not about voiding the mind and consciousness (as in Buddhism) but about *filling* your mind with the things of God.

EXERCISE: Practice meditating right now using Psalm 23.

- Choose one to two verses from the psalm to dwell on. Read them a few times over.
- Pick a phrase or word that sticks out and ponder it.
- Pray the passage back to God, committing to applying what you've gleaned.
- Offer praise to God for what you read.
- Call the phrase or word to mind as you go about your day and as you fall asleep at night.

Prayer[3]

> *When prayer is overlooked or appended as an afterthought to service, the power of God is often absent. It is dangerously easy to move away from dependence on God and to slip into the trap of self-reliance.*
>
> *Conformed to His Image, Revised Edition, 83*

Communicating with God—speaking *and* listening to him—is one of the great privileges of being his child. It should be the centerpiece of your spiritual journey.

However, it's easy to get locked into a rut of petitions (a "gimme, gimme" attitude). Prayer can and should be much richer than that, involving components of adoration, confession, renewal, thanksgiving, and intercession.

➤ How central is prayer to your life?

➤ Consider your daily routine. Are there times when you might purpose to carry on a dialogue with God *as you go about your activities?* Examples may include times when you're driving, waiting, or doing some mundane task that requires little thought (getting ready for the day, doing household chores, walking or exercising).

PRAY: Leave out your requests and instead simply adore God for who he is. Thank him for the privilege of being his child and of being invited into his presence because of the work of his Son on the cross.

Exchanged Life Spirituality

GRASPING OUR TRUE IDENTITY IN CHRIST

KEY VERSE

I have been crucified with Christ; and it is no longer I who live, but Christ lives in me; and the life which I now live in the flesh I live by faith in the Son of God, who loved me and gave Himself up for me.

Galatians 2:20

SUGGESTED READING

Conformed to His Image, Revised Edition, chapter 8

THE EXCHANGED LIFE

As Christians, we have received a new identity in Christ; we're new creations. And as Galatians 2:20 says, "It is no longer I who live, but Christ lives in me." This truth about our new identity is captured in the gospel of John with the phrase "you in Me, and I in you" (John 14:20; see also 17:21, 23). Over the years, some writers have referred to this in-Christ relationship as the "exchanged life." Although some exchanged life teachers have taken this idea too far, we will explore some of the biblical merits to this approach in this and the next session.

EXCHANGED LIFE: Christ's life for ours; death to our old self, and new life in Christ

Howard Hendricks describes the exchanged life as follows:

The life of Christ
reproduced in the believer
by the power of the Holy Spirit
in obedient response to the Word of God.[4]

➤ Read Romans 6:2–11 and Ephesians 2:5–6. Then write out how the passages describe the first two components of Hendricks' definition.

- "The life of Christ":

- "Reproduced in the believer":

OUR IDENTIFICATION WITH CHRIST

The Life of Christ	My Life (as a Believer)
Crucified and died	Crucified and died with Christ
Buried	Buried with Christ
Resurrected from the dead	Resurrected with Christ
Ascended into heaven	Seated in the heavenly places with Christ

Table 5

Contemplate the close identification with Christ that every believer has (as seen in the passage from Romans 6 that you just read and also as represented in table 5).

➤ How does this close identification change how you see yourself? How does it change your understanding of what Christ has done for you?

One implication of our in-Christ life is that without Christ, we are spiritually bankrupt. Only he can live the Christian life—in us and through us, as us (through the unique prism of our own personality). The same grace that brought us salvation also brings about our sanctification. We can't make ourselves holy; only he can do it. We see this "sanctification by grace" idea clearly in Paul's epistle to the Galatians.

➤ Read Galatians 3:2–3. Then consider: how much have you been depending on your efforts and resources to try to bring about your own sanctification? Do you see yourself as bringing something to the table or as coming empty-handed?

Although we can't be or do anything good without Christ living in us, neither are we off the hook. There's a divine-human dynamic. We're called to obedience—to put forth effort to cooperate with the Spirit in us. In this mysterious process, we retain the unique prism of our personality, through which he is then reflected and refracted.

➤ Read Galatians 5:16–26. What is the role of the Spirit in the life of the Christian?

➤ What's the difference between trying and training?

➤ Read John 14:18–21 and John 17:13–23. From these passages, say a prayer to God, such as, "I thank you for my identity in you, Jesus. Because you live, I also live. I pray that your people would be unified in you, that the world may know you sent Jesus Christ to save people from their sins and enjoy eternal life."

THE BATTLE THAT RAGES

Because of our in-Christ relationship, we have a new identity. Our truest self, our deepest self, is (somehow, mysteriously) now seated in the heavenly places with Christ (Ephesians 2:6). At the same time, we're engaged in a battle between our old and new selves as long as we're on our earthly sojourn. The process of our growth is gradual; growth is not a single event. Thus we live in a state of tension between the already and the not yet.

> *Fallen people sin because they are sinful by nature. It is not that they are sinners because they commit certain sins. . . . Unlike those who are fallen, those who are redeemed are able not to sin.*
>
> *Conformed to His Image, Revised Edition, 97*

In the quote, notice the phrase *"able not to sin."* The ordering of words is crucial: this is different than *"not able to sin."*

➤ Have you encountered what's known as "perfectionism"—the belief that Christians can no longer sin and therefore do not need to repent? If so, how does that teaching square with your experience? (Do you know any Christians who are no longer capable of sinning?)

This erroneous teaching of perfectionism not only is contrary to what we observe in day-to-day living but also is dismantled by Scripture, particularly by Paul in Romans 7–8.

> *Our deepest identity as spiritual beings has been transformed, but our redemption is not yet complete. . . . Then the inner and the outer will be perfectly integrated; we will be free from the power of sin, and our minds, emotions, and wills will be continually under the dominion of the Spirit of God. Until that time comes, we have been called to the task of allowing God to gradually conform our outer selves to the righteousness and holiness that were created in our inner selves at the moment of salvation. . . . A battle rages, but we must realize that the warfare is between the new creatures we have become in Christ (2 Corinthians 5:17) and the mortal remnants of the old people we were in Adam (Romans 5:12-21).*
>
> *Conformed to His Image, Revised Edition, 97-98*

➤ In what specific ways have you experienced the battle between your new self and old self?

Another error or extreme of exchanged life teaching assumes that as soon as we are saved and we have the Spirit in us, we're suddenly different, and permanent victory (over sin) is immediately ours. However, this is simply not the case, nor is it in line with Scripture. We are *progressively*, not suddenly, conformed to God's image.

➤ Read Romans 8:12–17. This passage makes clear that it's possible to be led by either the Spirit or the flesh. We are new creatures, but we still experience the pull of old beliefs, attitudes, and appetites as long as we're in the body. How have you experienced this pull, and in what areas of your life have you felt it most?

➤ When we wrestle with this pull, it can be easy for doubts to enter our minds, even to the point of doubting our salvation (especially if we deal with a certain sin over and over). In this case, we can turn to Scripture for hope and assurance. What hope do the words of Romans 8:31–39 offer?

Another term for the exchanged life is the "abiding life" (especially emphasized in the writings of Andrew Murray). This idea comes from John 15:1–8, where we see the in-Christ life described in terms of branches grafted into a vine (Jesus). To the extent that we abide in him, we will produce the fruit of his Spirit in us.

➤ Visualize a branch connected to a vine. Then write down some ways in which this imagery parallels our life in Christ. What is the branch's job? The vine's?

PRAY: Pray that you will abide in Jesus today, realizing that you can do nothing of lasting value apart from him (John 15:5).

> As branches of the true vine, we do not create life, but we receive it through our connection with the vine. The new life that flows in and through us is displayed in the fruit we bear, and this fruit not only nourishes others but also contains the seeds of its own reproduction.
>
> *Conformed to His Image, Revised Edition*, 93

OUR GOD-CREATED NEEDS

The battle between our old and new selves is a conflict we never totally escape on earth. Although the power of sin has been removed because of Christ's sacrifice on the cross, the presence of sin remains a reality until we leave this life for the next. This conflict is especially evident in the area of our physical and psychological needs.

In the next session, we'll further explore God's plan to meet our needs, but here we'll briefly consider these needs and why our knowledge of God and his character is so important in addressing them.

Our Needs

> We are inherently motivated to have our needs met, but it is extremely easy for us to be deceived into the world's thinking that they can be met in some place other than the hand of God. This can lead only to frustration, because no person, possession, or position can take the place of what God alone can do.
>
> *Conformed to His Image, Revised Edition*, 98

Besides the obvious physical needs that all humans have, we have three basic categories of psychological needs. If we seek to meet these in the wrong places, we fall into the same deceptions that non-Christians fall into, and ultimately are left feeling empty and restless.

➤ Take a look at table 6. Which psychological need or needs (love, acceptance, significance, identity, competence, fulfillment) do you most struggle with seeking to have filled in God alone?

HUMAN PSYCHOLOGICAL NEEDS AND HOW THEY ARE MET

Category of Psychological Need	Result If Met in Wrong Place	Leads To	Carried Further	Extreme Case
Love and acceptance	Appearance rejection	Feelings of insecurity	Sensuality and immorality	Perversion
Significance and identity	Personhood rejection	Feelings of inferiority	Materialism and greed	Theft
Competence and fulfillment	Performance rejection	Feelings of inadequacy	Excessive competition and aggression	Violence

Table 6

➤ Where do you (or where are you tempted to) try to fill that need or those needs?

➤ Look at the last three columns. Which, if any, of these consequences have you experienced?

God's Character and Plan

When we seek to get our needs met in the wrong places, we fall out of step with the Spirit in us (Galatians 5:25). We stop abiding in Christ and begin living in the flesh, just like nonbelievers. Although we may acknowledge God as the one who meets those needs *in theory,* our practice may tell another story.

> *God's character is fundamental to everything else. . . . The better we grasp the love and goodness of God's character, the less we will be tempted to think that he is carrying out his plans at our expense. It is always to our advantage to conform to his will, because it leads to our highest good.*
>
> *Conformed to His Image, Revised Edition, 95–96*

➤ Ponder the two key aspects of God's character, his love and his goodness, through the following verses. Are you clinging to these now, even in the face of adversities you may be facing?

God's Love

God so loved the world that he gave his one and only Son, that whoever believes in him shall not perish but have eternal life.

John 3:16 NIV

God is love.

1 John 4:8

. . . just as Christ loved the church and gave himself up for her.

Ephesians 5:25 NIV

God's Goodness (Kindness)

. . . so that in the ages to come He might show the surpassing riches of His grace in kindness toward us in Christ Jesus.

Ephesians 2:7

The Lord is gracious and merciful;
Slow to anger and great in lovingkindness.
The Lord is good to all,
And His mercies are over all His works.

Psalm 145:8-9

PRAY: Ask God to reveal to you his love and goodness. Then thank him for what he shows you.

Exchanged Life Spirituality

GOD'S PLAN TO MEET OUR NEEDS

> **KEY VERSES**
>
> He rescued us from the domain of darkness, and transferred us to the kingdom of His beloved Son, in whom we have redemption, the forgiveness of sins.
>
> *Colossians 1:13–14*
>
> **SUGGESTED READING**
>
> *Conformed to His Image, Revised Edition,* chapter 9

A SPIRITUAL FAMILY, BODY, AND HOUSE

Our redemption paves the way for a repaired relationship with God the Father, who has promised to meet the needs of his children. We discussed these needs (love and acceptance, significance and identity, and competence and fulfillment) in the previous session. Now we'll look at how these needs are fully met by God.

Our need *for unconditional love and acceptance* is fully met in our new *spiritual family.*

> When the fullness of the time came, God sent forth His Son . . . so that He might redeem those who were under the Law, that we might receive the adoption as sons.
>
> *Galatians 4:4–5*

The apostle Paul, in his letters to the Galatians and Ephesians, speaks of this family in terms of adoption.

➤ Read Galatians 4:4–7 and Ephesians 1:4–6. What changes occur when a person is adopted? How is this similar to what happens when we join our new, spiritual family?

➤ Does the prospect of belonging to a perfectly united, loving spiritual family—which cannot be broken in any permanent way—appeal to you? Why or why not?

God meets our need for lasting *significance and identity* by adjoining us to a *spiritual body*—a community, headed by Christ—that goes on forever. We're now part of something bigger than ourselves.

> God has so composed the body, giving more abundant honor to that member which lacked, so that there may be no division in the body, but that the members may have the same care for one another. And if one member suffers, all the members suffer with it; if one member is honored, all the members rejoice with it.
>
> 1 Corinthians 12:24-26

➤ How does participation as one individual member of the body of Christ meet our need for significance and identity?

➢ Read 1 Corinthians 12:12–27, noticing especially verse 25. God's plan for his body (the church) is not division among members but, rather, mutual care for one another. What examples of mutual care have you observed? What examples of division have you observed?

➢ How should we view brokenness in his body? What can we do it about it?

> Coming to Him as to a living stone which has been rejected by men, but is choice and precious in the sight of God, you also, as living stones, are being built up as a spiritual house for a holy priesthood, to offer up spiritual sacrifices acceptable to God through Jesus Christ.
>
> 1 Peter 2:4-5

God fully meets our need for lasting *competence and fulfillment* through our part in God's *spiritual house* (or *temple*). First Peter 2:4–5 compares our life in Christ to being part of a building of living stones, with Christ as the cornerstone. (This concept is also in Ephesians 2:20.) In this house, we each have a role to play and gifts to use.

➢ Read 1 Peter 2:4–5. What is the purpose of this spiritual house, and what materials are used to build it?

OUR RESPONSE: A THREEFOLD PROCESS

> *God's truth is designed not merely to inform us but also to transform us.*
>
> *Conformed to His Image, Revised Edition,* 107

God's Word reveals a three-step process for responding to God's plan to meet our needs: knowing, reckoning, and yielding. Paul reveals this process clearly in Romans 6.

1. *Knowing* (Romans 6:3–10)—understanding the truth of our identity in Christ, based on what God says because of Christ's crucifixion, not on what we or others say about us
2. *Reckoning* (Romans 6:11)—regarding this truth to be so in our lives (our co-crucifixion with Christ)
3. *Yielding* (Romans 6:12–14)—acting on what we know and believe to be true about our identity in Christ

EXERCISE: Practice this three-step process.

1. Pick a truth from Scripture that you have difficulty believing and living out. (Hint: Choose one of the "Who God Says You Are" statements from session 3.) Then answer the following three questions.

   Who do I say I am?

   Who do other people say I am?

   Who does God say I am?

Reckon yourselves to be dead indeed to sin, but alive to God in Christ Jesus our Lord.

Romans 6:11 NKJV

2. Reckon the third answer (God's) to be true. Don't worry about your feelings; simply focus on what God says is true, and trust and honor him in that.

3. Seek to apply this truth in your day-to-day thoughts, words, and actions. Use the space here to brainstorm a couple ways you can do so.

Your real, new self . . . will not come as long as you are looking for it. It will come when you are looking for Him.

C. S. Lewis, *Mere Christianity*

GRACE-BASED LIVING

The goal of the Christian life is to become more and more in practice who you are in your position in Christ. You should have an increasing realization that:

Jesus Christ gave his life for you (*salvation*)
so that he could give his life to you (*sanctification*)
so that he could live his life through you (*service*)

In our lives, Christ is to increase while we're to decrease (John 3:30). We're to grow in grace—living by grace rather than by works.

Two possible extremes:

LEGALISM: do-what-you-have-to-do mentality; entails striving in the effort of the flesh to achieve a human standard of righteousness; often evident by a list of (unspoken) dos and don'ts

LICENSE: do-what-you-want-to-do mentality; stems from taking God's grace for granted and leads to downplaying the consequences of sin; often evident in the bending of God's moral law in one's own favor under the claim of Christian grace and liberty

The balance (struck in the in-Christ life):

LIBERTY: true freedom to do as Christ pleases; understands that growth in Christ is an inside-out process

➤ Do you tend toward either legalism or license? If so, which one?

➤ In what specific ways does this tendency manifest itself in your life?

To preach devotion first, and blessing second, is to reverse God's order, and preach law, not grace.

William Newell

There is a significant difference between human efforts to do things for Jesus and inviting him to live and manifest his life through us.

Conformed to His Image, Revised Edition, 113

The Christian life involves effort, but there is a difference between making efforts for Jesus out of our own power and asking him to live in and through us. Look at table 7, and then assess whether you are living more by grace or by law.

LAW-BASED VERSUS GRACE-BASED LIVING

	Law	**Grace**
Says	Do	Done
Emphasizes	What we do	What God does
Lives out of	The flesh (self-life)	The Spirit (Christ's life)
Draws on	Our resources	God's resources
Deals with	External rules, regulations, standards	Inner heart attitude
Primary focus	Ought to, should, must	Want to
Creates	Bondage, duty, obligation	Freedom
Lives life from the	Outside in	Inside out
Declares	Do in order to be	You are; therefore do
Produces	Guilt and condemnation	Acceptance and security
Leads to	Defeat	Victory

Table 7

➢ Grace-based living doesn't eliminate the need for spiritual disciplines but contextualizes them. How can these two things—grace and discipline—abide together in a Christian's life?

➢ Ponder this idea at the crux of the exchanged life: *Christ became what he was not so that we might become what we were not. Because he became sin for us, we become the righteousness of God* (2 Corinthians 5:21). What are your thoughts on these truths?

PRAY: Pray for any areas in which you need to walk by grace instead of by law, and any areas in which you need to reckon certain truths to be true. Pray too for any areas in which you may be taking God's grace for granted.

Motivated Spirituality

WHY DO WE DO WHAT WE DO?

KEY VERSES

Simon Peter answered Him, "Lord, to whom shall we go? You have words of eternal life. We have believed and have come to know that You are the Holy One of God."

John 6:68–69

SUGGESTED READING

Conformed to His Image, Revised Edition, chapter 10

MOTIVATION IN THE CHRISTIAN LIFE

Humans are creatures of desire, set on course by various motivators. Even the believer is motivated by competing factors. The apostle Paul wrote much about the struggle of motivation (or desire) versus practice in Romans 7:14–25 and Galatians 5:16–26. Read these two passages now.

➤ What advantage does the believer have over the unbeliever in (1) understanding our underlying motivators, and (2) being controlled by these motivators?

Look at the fruit of the Spirit listed in Galatians 5:22–23. Consider what the opposite of each of these might be and fill in the second column of table 8.

OPPOSITES OF THE FRUIT OF THE SPIRIT

Fruit of the Spirit	Opposite
Love	
Joy	
Peace	
Patience	
Kindness	
Goodness	
Faithfulness	
Gentleness	
Self-control	

Table 8

➤ Where do you see these opposite motivators in the world around you?

➤ When you are tempted to succumb to such motivators, how can you choose instead to walk by the Spirit?

Biblical Motivators

We are all motivated to act in certain ways based on our needs for security, significance, and fulfillment. We will choose either the world or Christ as we look to satisfy those needs. The following biblical motivators become more real and internal as we progress in spiritual maturity.

1. *No other options*—Christ is the only one who can satisfy us (we have nowhere better to turn)
2. *Fear*—both positive (fear of God) and negative (fear of consequences)
3. *Love and gratitude*—stemming from God's grace
4. *Rewards*—incentives for faithfulness
5. *Identity in Christ*—the foundation of who we are as a new creation
6. *Purpose and hope*—stemming from the plans and promises of God
7. *Longing for God*—a deep desire to be with God both now and in the future

➤ Of these seven biblical motivators, which do you currently find most compelling?

➤ Can you think of a season in which you found a different option most motivating? If so, what caused the difference—life circumstances, level of understanding, experience, or something else?

➤ Does the reality of multiple motivators working more effectively at different times or in different areas of your life teach you anything about who you are? About God?

MOTIVATOR 1: NO OTHER OPTIONS

Without God and immortality, our life and indeed that of the whole human race is futile. . . . We may have the illusion of meaning because others are still around, but in the long run, all of us will disappear, and our work and sacrifice will make no difference to an impersonal and indifferent cosmos.

Conformed to His Image, Revised Edition, 123

"No other options" is a negative motivator, referring to the reality that no one and nothing else offers what Christ offers—only he satisfies, and only the Christian world-view provides the answers we're looking for.

➤ In what way(s) does this motivator inspire obedience?

➤ In what way(s) does this motivator help combat dryness, doubt, or discouragement?

Peter's confession in John 6:68–69 is a concise statement of the Christian worldview and an acknowledgement of the bankruptcy of other views. What would become of the following critical elements of one's worldview if there were not an infinite, personal God beyond and in the universe?

• Meaning:

• Morality:

- Purpose:

- Destiny:

MOTIVATOR 2: FEAR

Fear, another common motivator, can be positive or negative, biblical or unbiblical. Revelation 1:17 tells us that the apostle John, upon seeing Christ, "fell at His feet like a dead man," needing to be told by Jesus, "Do not be afraid." Yet this same man, the disciple whom Jesus loved (John 13:23), wrote, "There is *no fear* in love; but perfect love casts out fear" (1 John 4:18, emphasis added).

➤ What do these verses teach about appropriate responses to God?

➤ Look up the following verses that mention the fear of the Lord. What does the fear of the Lord lead to?

- Exodus 20:20   _____
- Deuteronomy 5:29   _____
- Deuteronomy 6:24   _____
- 2 Kings 17:39   _____
- Psalm 40:3   _____
- Psalm 111:10   _____
- Psalm 128:4   _____
- Psalm 147:11   _____
- Proverbs 1:7   _____
- Proverbs 10:27   _____
- Proverbs 14:26   _____
- Proverbs 16:6   _____

- Ecclesiastes 8:12–13 _____
- Malachi 4:2 _____
- 2 Corinthians 5:11 _____
- 2 Corinthians 7:1 _____
- Revelation 15:4 _____

FEAR: a sense of awe, of majesty, of the reality that the mystery we call God is one who has claims on us that are transcendent, and that everything—our life, our deportment, all of our well-being—is utterly dependent on his good pleasure

➤ This week, what will you do to cultivate a sense of awe (fear) of the God you cannot see, so that it will overwhelm your fear of people you can see?

It may help to concentrate on these three areas:

- Your very life (Acts 17:28; Colossians 1:16–17)
- Your deportment—your demeanor and behavior (Colossians 1:9–12)
- Your well-being (Ecclesiastes 8:12–13)

Motivated Spirituality

LOVE, GRATITUDE, AND REWARDS

KEY VERSES

Beloved, now we are children of God, and it has not appeared as yet what we will be. We know that when He appears, we will be like Him, because we will see Him just as He is. And everyone who has this hope fixed on Him purifies himself, just as He is pure.

1 John 3:2–3

SUGGESTED READING

Conformed to His Image, Revised Edition, chapter 11

MOTIVATOR 3: LOVE AND GRATITUDE

Love

The Bible deepens our understanding of love both for God and for one another by revealing that God loves us before we love him. It is out of his love that we are able to love others (1 John 4:8–10).

➤ How does the love of Christ humble us without degrading us and elevate us without inflating us?

➤ In Romans, Paul expounds on the *abundant* and *conquering* love of Christ. Study the following two passages and make a list of adjectives describing Christ's love. Try to list at least twelve.

Hope does not disappoint, because the love of God has been poured out within our hearts through the Holy Spirit who was given to us.

For while we were still helpless, at the right time Christ died for the ungodly. For one will hardly die for a righteous man; though perhaps for the good man someone would dare even to die. But God demonstrates His own love toward us, in that while we were yet sinners, Christ died for us. Much more then, having now been justified by His blood, we shall be saved from the wrath of God through Him. For if while we were enemies we were reconciled to God through the death of His Son, much more, having been reconciled, we shall be saved by His life. And not only this, but we also exult in God through our Lord Jesus Christ, through whom we have now received the reconciliation.

Romans 5:5–11

Who will separate us from the love of Christ? Will tribulation, or distress, or persecution, or famine, or nakedness, or peril, or sword? Just as it is written,

> "For Your sake we are being put to death all day long;
> We were considered as sheep to be slaughtered."

But in all these things we overwhelmingly conquer through Him who loved us. For I am convinced that neither death, nor life, nor angels, nor principalities, nor things present, nor things to come, nor powers, nor height, nor depth, nor any other created thing, will be able to separate us from the love of God, which is in Christ Jesus our Lord.

Romans 8:35–39

Adjectives describing Christ's love:

Exploring what God has written in his Word about his love helps us align toward this divine love. Use the list you just created as an aid to your worship and a guide to your prayers. The following two questions can help assess where you are in your spiritual journey with respect to grasping and entering into God's divine love.

➤ Do you love God more for himself than for his gifts and benefits?

➤ Do you generally seek his glory and honor more than your own?

➤ If you answered no to one or both questions, do you *want* your answers to be yes?

➤ Committing to Jesus comes with a cost, for the world will hate those who love and follow him. This prompts a final question: Are you willing to pay the price? (See John 14:15.)

PRAY: We're all at risk of slipping into wrong motivations. Regardless of where you are in your spiritual journey, pray and ask the Lord to kindle (or continue to grow) your desire to draw nearer to him and to commit to him whatever the cost. Ask him to increase your love for him so that you will live with your mind and heart set on him.

Gratitude

Gratitude, or thanksgiving, is linked to love in that both mark the heart of one who realizes all that God is and all that he has done for us.

> One act of thanksgiving when things go wrong with us is worth a thousand thanks when things are agreeable to our inclinations.
>
> John of Ávila

➤ Consider John of Ávila's observation in light of Paul's admonishment "In everything give thanks" (1 Thessalonians 5:18). For what reason(s) can you give thanks even in the midst of failure, heartache, pain, or trouble?

Love and gratitude are choices, and we would do well to view them as spiritual disciplines because they each grow the more they're practiced. You must do more than simply *hope* to be more grateful; you must *train* yourself to be more grateful. We offer three exercises to help you train your heart to focus on God and renew your mind with a spirit of gratitude.

EXERCISE: Audience of One.[5] It's easy to live our lives before the wrong audience. People are right in front of us, and their demands are incessant. But to walk with God, we must play to him as our audience, making it our single-minded goal to please him (2 Corinthians 5:9) and to live *coram deo* (before the heart of God) rather than to impress people or win their praise. Free yourself from bondage to the opinions, agendas, and expectations of others by asking yourself the following question each time you are about to make a decision: "Am I now seeking the favor of men, or of God?" (Galatians 1:10). List the decisions you have to make and reflect on how you will focus on pleasing God rather than people for each one.

- Upcoming decisions and how I'll focus on pleasing God when I make them:

EXERCISE: The Hard Thanksgiving. Paul, in 1 Thessalonians 5:18, says we're to give thanks—not in some, not in most, but in *all* circumstances. The word he uses for thanksgiving is *eucharisteō* (from which we get the word *Eucharist*—one term for the Lord's Supper or Communion). Sometimes *eucharisteō* comes easily, as when we get good news or something exciting happens to us. But there's also a "hard thanksgiving." This is what we do in circumstances that, in our limited view, seem difficult or less than desirable. Think about your life right now. Do you need to offer God a hard thanksgiving for something? If so, do it now and several more times this week, asking him to help you see that circumstance as a temporary part of living on this earth. Ask God to use this situation to help you lean on him more, draw closer to him, and welcome his presence into more of your life.

- Circumstance for which I will give a hard thanksgiving:

EXERCISE: Four Areas of Gratitude. God turns the difficulties of life into a redemptive tool when our gaze is fixed on him instead of on our ourselves. Cultivate a sense of gratitude for the goodness of life and the tender mercies of God that you tend to overlook, by thinking about something you're grateful for in each of the following four categories. Record the thing you're grateful for in each category, and then thank God daily for those four things.

- The glory of God's creation:

- A material blessing:

- A relational blessing (someone in your life):

- A spiritual blessing:

MOTIVATOR 4: REWARDS

Rewards is one of the most misunderstood motivators as well as one of the most over- .
looked by many Christians.

> *It's easy to lip-synch in the chorus of life, but each of us will have to sing solo
> before God.*
>
> Conformed to His Image, Revised Edition, 133

Condition for Rewards

Review the parables in the following passages. What do you learn from these teachings of Jesus about the condition for rewards?

- Matthew 20:1–16

- Luke 19:11–27

Many have a mistaken view that the fear of loss and the hope of reward are not legitimate, biblical motivators. But the Bible speaks of rewards in a positive way.

➢ Each of the following sentences represents a false view regarding rewards. Review these erroneous statements, and correct the view they express so they align with biblical teaching (based on the Scripture given).[6]

1. False view: Pursuing rewards is a selfish motivation.

   Corrected view (Hebrews 11:6):

2. False view: I'm not motivated by rewards; heaven is reward enough.

   Corrected view (Romans 6:23):

3. False view: Fear of loss and hope of reward are not legitimate motivators.

   Corrected view (1 Corinthians 9:24–25):

Areas of Rewards

While we don't have great specificity as to the nature and content of future rewards, there are four areas in which we get glimpses of heaven.

1. Varying responsibilities and spheres of authority in God's kingdom (Luke 19:17–19; Revelation 3:21; 5:10; 20:4)
2. Varying degrees of reflecting and displaying God's glory (Daniel 12:2–3)
3. Richness of relational rewards (Luke 16:9; 1 Thessalonians 2:19–20)
4. Capacity for relating to God (1 Corinthians 13:12)

➤ The last chapter in the Bible contains a description of our future hope. Read Revelation 22:3–5 and see how many of the four areas of rewards you identify.

There will no longer be any curse; and the throne of God and of the Lamb will be in it, and His bond-servants will serve Him; they will see His face, and His name will be on their foreheads. And there will no longer be any night; and they will not have need of the light of a lamp nor the light of the sun, because the Lord God will illumine them; and they will reign forever and ever.

Revelation 22:3–5

Motivated Spirituality

IDENTITY, PURPOSE AND HOPE, AND LONGING FOR GOD

KEY VERSE

If I go and prepare a place for you, I will come again and receive you to Myself, that where I am, there you may be also.

John 14:3

SUGGESTED READING

Conformed to His Image, Revised Edition, chapter 12

MOTIVATOR 5: IDENTITY IN CHRIST

Issues of identity cut to the core of our being and can become for us a source of demotivation. Consider the following major sources of identity problems.

- Failing to understand our origins
- Being misunderstood by those around us
- Being mislabeled
- Having misaligned goals and timelines

- Choosing poor role models
- Having no vision for the future

➢ How does 1 John 3:1–3 address these issues?

See how great a love the Father has bestowed on us, that we would be called children of God; and such we are. For this reason the world does not know us, because it did not know Him. Beloved, now we are children of God, and it has not appeared as yet what we will be. We know that when He appears, we will be like Him, because we will see Him just as He is. And everyone who has this hope fixed on Him purifies himself, just as He is pure.

1 John 3:1–3

➢ In addition to identity in Christ, which other of the seven biblical motivators (introduced and listed in session 11 on page 74) are present in this passage?

➢ How does this passage deal with identity issues across time (past, present, and future)?

Scripture does not command us to feel the truth but to believe it.
Conformed to His Image, Revised Edition, 141

The truths of Scripture are greater than our feelings. Consider again 1 John 3:1–3. List the truths in the passage that help combat the following feelings of being:

- Unloved

- Unimportant

- Unvalued

- Unknown

- Ungodly

- Unworthy

- Unclean

MOTIVATOR 6: PURPOSE AND HOPE

Purpose

➤ Read Mark 10:45, Luke 19:10, and John 17:4. What do these verses reveal about the purpose of Jesus' life on earth?

➤ How does knowing Jesus' purpose inform your life purpose and pursuit?

Failing to intentionally pursue your purpose can result in loss of the joy, fulfillment, and service that Christ has called you to. Merely hoping that you will one day stumble upon your life purpose is not the sort of purpose and hope this session is encouraging! Consider the following training exercise to help you identify God's purpose and calling for your life.[7]

EXERCISE: Calling and Purpose. It's easy to allow the world to mold us into its image rather than allowing God to shape us and our life purpose. All Christians are called to love God completely, ourselves correctly, and others compassionately, and we do so specifically through the unique prism of our life context, personality, and resources.

- Below, write out how you view your personal calling in light of your general calling as a Christian. (This calling should reflect a lifelong vocation that extends beyond present career boundaries and life circumstances.)

- Review your calling twice a day so you will invest your time wisely:
   - *At the beginning of each day* review your plan for the day. Is there anything you should cut out or make time for in light of your calling?
   - *At the end of each day* review how the day went. Did anything crop up that you should have turned down? Were there any opportunities God put in your path that were in line with his calling for you but weren't part of your planned agenda? Note these incidents and how they came about.

Hope

Hope can be seen as a bridge between purpose and longing for God. This is because both hope and purpose move us toward long-term gain, while both hope and longing aspire to that which is yet to be realized.

> The perfection of hope lies not in achieving what it hopes for, but in embracing its standard, namely the God on whose help it relies.
>
> Thomas Aquinas, *Summa Theologiæ*

➤ In what ways can hope be virtuous even though that hope may not be fulfilled or realized in this life? (Consider 1 John 3:3 and the quote from Aquinas above.)

> Sanctify Christ as Lord in your hearts, always being ready to make a defense to everyone who asks you to give an account for the hope that is in you, yet with gentleness and reverence.
>
> 1 Peter 3:15

One effect of hope is that it externally witnesses to others (as 1 Peter 3:15 indicates). While we've focused on the motivational factors for your spiritual formation, we also highlighted that there's no act that begins with the love of God that doesn't end with the love of others. As you review the seven biblical motivators again, how might each of these be used as an evangelistic opportunity when others notice these motivations in you?

1. No other options

2. Fear

3. Love and gratitude

4. Rewards

5. Identity in Christ

6. Purpose and hope

7. Longing for God

MOTIVATOR 7: LONGING FOR GOD

In the Psalms, longing for God is often described in terms of thirst.

> As the deer pants for the water brooks,
> So my soul pants for You, O God.
> My soul thirsts for God, for the living God;
> When shall I come and appear before God?
>
> Psalm 42:1–2

O God, You are my God; I shall seek You earnestly;

My soul thirsts for You, my flesh yearns for You,

In a dry and weary land where there is no water.

Psalm 63:1

➢ What, if anything, have you desired in a way comparable to the thirst described in these two psalms? Have you experienced a desire for God in this way?

➢ Longing is probably the least commonly experienced spiritual source of motivation. Why do you think that is so?

➢ How is this seventh motivator related to the other six we've reviewed?

The video session concluded with a mention of Paul's prayers for the Ephesians, Philippians, and Colossians. Incorporating these into your prayer time can be a rewarding exercise that fosters your longing for God. These prayers are part of a Spiritual Renewal Card collection, two of which are found on the next page.[8]

PAUL'S FOUR LIFE-CHANGING PRAYERS

[I ask] that the God of our Lord Jesus Christ, the Father of glory, may give to you a spirit of wisdom and of revelation in the knowledge of Him. I pray that the eyes of your heart may be enlightened, so that you will know what is the hope of His calling, what are the riches of the glory of His inheritance in the saints, and what is the surpassing greatness of His power toward us who believe. (EPH. 1:17–19a)

[May the Father] grant you, according to the riches of His glory, to be strengthened with power through His Spirit in the inner man, so that Christ may dwell in your hearts through faith; and that you, being rooted and grounded in love, may be able to comprehend with all the saints what is the breadth and length and height and depth, and to know the love of Christ which surpasses knowledge, that you may be filled up to all the fullness of God. (EPH. 3:16–19)

Figure 2

PAUL'S FOUR LIFE-CHANGING PRAYERS

And this I pray, that your love may abound still more and more in real knowledge and all discernment, so that you may approve the things that are excellent, in order to be sincere and blameless until the day of Christ; having been filled with the fruit of righteousness which comes through Jesus Christ, to the glory and praise of God. (PHIL. 1:9–11)

[I ask] that you may be filled with the knowledge of His will in all spiritual wisdom and understanding, so that you will walk in a manner worthy of the Lord, to please Him in all respects, bearing fruit in every good work and increasing in the knowledge of God; strengthened with all power, according to His glorious might, for the attaining of all steadfastness and patience; joyously giving thanks to the Father, who has qualified us to share in the inheritance of the saints in Light. (COL. 1:9b–12)

Figure 3

Devotional Spirituality

OUR IMAGE OF GOD

KEY VERSE

Great is the LORD, and highly to be praised,
And His greatness is unsearchable.

Psalm 145:3

SUGGESTED READING

Conformed to His Image, Revised Edition, chapter 13

THE LIFE OF THE MIND

Devotional spirituality relates to growth in intimacy with God. Closeness to God, in turn, has much to do with the focus of our thoughts and desires.

> What comes into our minds when we think about God is the most important thing about us.
>
> A. W. Tozer

➤ What comes into your mind when you think about God?

➢ Would you have answered that question differently in years past? If so, what changed?

While you may not be able to control every thought that comes into your mind, there is a difference between passively giving in to the default position of the world and actively following the disciplined practice of training your mind.

➢ The corresponding video session posed the question, "Do you nourish great thoughts about the living God?" List your habits of nourishment (for example, memorizing Scripture, telling others what God has done for you, or reflecting on God's blessings in your life). Then list your habits of neglect. Consider what adjustments you might want to make in terms of your priorities, schedule, or fellowship.

GROWTH THROUGH WORSHIP

The more we come to know and love God, the more our intentions and aspirations will center on him instead of on ourselves. Our goal is to become more like Christ, because we resemble what we worship.

> *We steadily become conformed to what we most love and admire. . . . If our heart's desire is fixed on something in this world, it becomes idolatrous and soul-corrupting. But if we draw our life from loving communion with the caring, radiant, majestic, and unfathomable Being who formed us for himself, our souls become noble as they grow in conformity to his character.*
>
> *Conformed to His Image, Revised Edition, 152–53*

➤ There will always be things that compete for our love and admiration. What pleasures currently compete for your love and admiration? (Note: These won't necessarily be *bad* things, although some could be. Consider activities, habits, physical things, and people you enjoy or are devoted to.)

➤ If you were to pursue that list in lieu of devotion to God, in what ways would those pleasures shape your life? (Consider various aspects, such as the life of the mind, your relationships, and short- and long-term consequences.)

➤ Your view of worship may be too narrow, restricted either to certain activities on Sunday or to that which seems overtly religious. Consider the following quote by William Temple. Are there areas in your life which you've not opened to the worship of your Creator?

Worship is the submission of all our nature to God. It is the quickening of conscience by his holiness; the nourishment of mind with his truth; the purifying of imagination by his beauty; the opening of the heart to his love; the surrender of will to his purpose—and all of this gathered up in adoration, the most selfless emotion of which our nature is capable and therefore the chief remedy for that self-centeredness which is our original sin and the source of all actual sin.

William Temple, *Readings in St. John's Gospel*

➤ We are shaped by our aspirations and conformed by our pursuits and intentions. This video session posed the question, "What do you want more than anything else?" We've seen this question before (in session 7). In the space here, write out what you honestly want. Feel free to amend your previous answer if anything has changed.

PRAY: An honest assessment of your desires doesn't need to result in discouragement or despair. If our chief desire isn't God, then *wanting to want him* is a noble pursuit. Make that the object of prayer.

REFLECTING ON REVELATION

The proper worship of God depends not just on your desire for devotion but on an accurate understanding of your object of worship.

- Why are the *who, why,* and *how* of worship all important?

- What are the consequences of a less-than-accurate understanding of who God is?

Though God in his essence is a mystery beyond our comprehension, he has revealed himself to us through his *world, word, works,* and *ways.*

God's World

Since the creation of the world His invisible attributes, His eternal power and divine nature, have been clearly seen, being understood through what has been made, so that [people] are without excuse.

Romans 1:20

➤ In what way does Romans 1:20 speak to both the mystery and the knowability of God?

➤ If we could comprehend God completely in our human minds, what would that mean about the nature of God?

➤ What does God's revelation to us of some things about himself tell us about his nature?

Careful consideration of God's world may be the most neglected component of devotional spirituality. We encounter the created world daily, but most of us fail to meditate often on the marvels of both the macrocosm and microcosm.

EXERCISE: Consider immersing yourself in God's revealed world in one of the following ways.[9]

- Find a place where you can sit back and stare at the stars; give yourself opportunity for awe as you ponder the God who knows their name and number (Psalm 147:4).
- Visit NASA's *Image of the Day* webpage (*https://apod.nasa.gov*) to learn more about the universe beyond what your eyes can see—worlds unknown to other generations but always known to God.
- Explore your own back yard with a hand lens (loupe) and a flashlight to observe otherwise overlooked patterns and colors.

God's Word

Read Psalm 19:7–11 to discover the transforming power of God's Word.

> The law of the Lord is perfect, restoring the soul;
> The testimony of the Lord is sure, making wise the simple.

The precepts of the Lord are right, rejoicing the heart;

The commandment of the Lord is pure, enlightening the eyes.

The fear of the Lord is clean, enduring forever;

The judgments of the Lord are true; they are righteous altogether.

They are more desirable than gold, yes, than much fine gold;

Sweeter also than honey and the drippings of the honeycomb.

Moreover, by them Your servant is warned;

In keeping them there is great reward.

Psalm 19:7-11

Notice that this psalm offers both descriptors for God's Word as well as the results of his revelation in our lives. Use table 9 to record these descriptions and corresponding revelations. (We've provided an example to get you started.)

Verse	Description	Result
19:7	The law of the Lord is perfect	It restores the soul

Table 9

> ➤ God's revelation in his written Word offers opportunity not only for *informing* you but also for *transforming* you. Look at the table you just created on Psalm 19. Which areas speak to this idea of transformation?

> ➤ Consider the contrast between informational and formational reading in table 10, both of which are important in your pursuit of loving God. Do you tend to approach Scripture in one of these two ways more than the other? If so, how might you achieve a healthier balance?

INFORMATION VERSUS FORMATION: TWO PURPOSES IN BIBLE READING

Informational Reading	Formational Reading
Seeks to cover as much as possible	Focuses on small portions
A linear process	An in-depth process
Seeks to master the text	Allows the text to master us
The text as an object to use	The text as a subject that shapes us
Analytical, critical, judgmental approach	Humble, submissive, willing, loving approach
Problem-solving mentality	Openness to mystery

Table 10

God's Works

God invites us to "come and see the works of God, who is awesome in His deeds toward the sons of men" (Psalm 66:5). A review of God's works is a nourishing reminder of who he is.

Make a list of God's works that will help you recall the power, faithfulness, and love of your Maker. Consider those works present in your personal life, works made known to the public, and works promised for the future.

- Personal works

- Public works

- Promised works

God's Ways

God's world, word, and works all speak to the ways in which he operates in love toward you.

EXERCISE: Using a separate piece of paper or a journal, record a personal history of God's providential care for you by reviewing and remembering the ways in which he has revealed himself to you. After recording this history:

- Take note of any patterns that you see.
- Pray for a greater consciousness of God's ways and for continued faithfulness as he reveals himself in your life.
- Consider how your life might have been different if things had gone your way instead of God's.

Devotional Spirituality

THE CONTEMPLATIVE WAY

KEY VERSE

When You said, "Seek My face," my heart said to You, "Your face, O Lord, I shall seek."

Psalm 27:8

SUGGESTED READING

Conformed to His Image, Revised Edition, chapter 14

CONTEMPLATIVE CONTROVERSY

For many, the contemplative way (a focus on experiencing the love of God through intense introspection) connotes an unmoored, potentially dangerous approach to God. Answer the following questions according to your current understanding of contemplative spirituality.

➢ In what way(s) might contemplation be negative?

➤ In what way(s) might contemplation be positive?

➤ Some terms commonly associated with contemplative practices include "mystical," "esoteric," and "Eastern." How do such associations influence your thoughts on contemplative spirituality?

Where to Begin?

➤ Contemplative spirituality might not be the best starting place for growing in Christ because of the significant discernment it requires. Does this make sense to you, or does it cause alarm?

➤ Can you think of an instance in which your initial understanding of Christian doctrine changed as you gave it more thought and did more research?

➤ On the flip side, is there an instance in which your initial concern or reservations about a teaching or practice was proven right as you dug deeper?

The Primacy of Scripture

> *Contemplation must always be tethered to the truth of the Word. Contemplation is not an introspective New Age practice of **altered consciousness** or **voiding the mind** of content. Engagement in **bogus mysticism** and introspection leads at best to **sloppy sentimentality** and **self-delusion** and at worst to **demonic influences**.*
> *Conformed to His Image, Revised Edition,* 164, emphases added

➤ For each of the descriptors listed in table 11, consider its opposite. Then look up the corresponding verses to consider how this opposite *could* be tethered to Scripture. Use these Scriptures as sources of contemplation as you read them.

BIBLICAL CONTEMPLATION CONTRASTED

Descriptor	Opposite	Scripture
Altered consciousness	Renewing the mind	Romans 12:2
Voiding the mind	Filling the mind	Philippians 4:8
Bogus mysticism	Partaking in the divine nature	2 Peter 1:2–4
Sloppy sentimentality	Recognition of God's faithfulness in the past and for our future	Hebrews 11:39–12:3
Self-delusion	Full assurance	Colossians 2:2–4
Demonic influences	Spirit-filled	Ephesians 5:18

Table 11

➤ How does Jesus' statement that "true worshipers will worship the Father in spirit and truth" (John 4:23) apply to contemplative practice?

Not for You?

➤ Perhaps more than other disciplines, contemplative practice is for many people a no-go from the start. It's assumed to be a practice for those of certain personalities, temperaments, or abilities. What would happen if we approached other aspects of spiritual formation with this attitude?

One of the goals of the contemplative way is the *development of passion and longing for God*. This means that contemplative spirituality is neither *instantaneous* nor *ingrained*.

PRAY: Pray through the following:

- God, teach me to develop my passion and longing for you rather than simply assuming that this longing will develop in some automatic way in me one day.
- God, grant me understanding and joy in this gradual development of passion for you; may I enjoy the process of drawing nearer and nearer to your presence.
- God, empower me to cultivate habits of intimacy by pursuing and responding to your gracious initiatives.
- God, give me the grace of holy desire.

THE EXPERIENTIAL WAY OF THE HEART

Scripture invites us beyond a mere intellectual commitment to the knowledge of the things of God (though intellectual commitment is vital). God invites us to know him in a relational, experiential way that encompasses all of our being (this is the greatest commandment). Consider the following verse.

> O taste and see that the LORD is good.
>
> Psalm 34:8

- What does this imagery—to taste and see—teach us about God?

- What does it teach us about the possibilities for our relationship with him?

Another psalm, Psalm 73, describes our relationship with God. Read Psalm 73, paying careful attention to verses 21–28. Then consider the following questions.

- What does this psalm teach about the heart?

- How does the heart's disposition affect the mind?

- What does this passage teach about God's presence?

- What does this passage teach about desire?

DETACHMENT AND DESIRE

There is a concerned guide, a knowing one, who attracts the attention of the wanderer, who calls out to him that he should take care. That guide is remorse. He is not so quick of foot as the indulgent imagination, which is the servant of desire. He is not so strongly built as the victorious intention. He comes on slowly afterwards. He grieves. But he is a sincere and faithful friend.

Søren Kierkegaard

Our journey toward God is often a journey away from lesser desires. The contemplative tradition calls for *compunction,* a sorrowful realization of selfish interests. Compunction, in turn, calls for *detachment* from our temporal desires. This detachment is both caused by and enhances our attachment to Christ.

Study the following verses, which speak to detachment and desire, and then answer the questions that follow: Matthew 10:37–39; 16:24–27; 2 Corinthians 5:1–9; and Hebrews 12:1–2.

- How would you characterize the various objects of desire mentioned in these verses?

- What challenges present themselves in pursuing Christ instead of these desires?

- What are the costs and rewards of obedience and disobedience in these areas?

- What habit, schedule, or priority do you need to adjust in order to align it with godly desires?

A series of Latin phrases describes the journey of the heart:

compunctio cordis (compunction of heart)
intentio cordis (intention of heart)
puritas cordis (purity of heart)

- How is each of these concepts a necessary component of your spiritual journey?

- What do you observe about the sequence in which these phrases are presented?

- How might this sequence apply to an area of struggle for you?

Dryness and Darkness

> *We must stop measuring the quality of our times of prayer and meditation by how well we feel during them, since difficult and apparently fruitless times of prayer may contribute more to our development than times of consolation and enthusiasm.*
>
> *Conformed to His Image, Revised Edition, 170*

➢ Does this quote surprise you in regard to contemplative prayer?

➢ Do you tend to judge the successfulness of your prayer time according to your feelings?

Consider the following enemies of spiritual progress. When we are defeated by these enemies, God may lead us through seasons of dryness and darkness to dislodge us from illusion and complacency. Identify areas in which you struggle.

- Entanglement

- Double-mindedness

- Compromise

- Complacency

PRAY: Spend some time now and throughout this week praying over the area(s) in which you struggle.

Devotional Spirituality

THE PRACTICE OF SACRED READING

KEY VERSE

His delight is in the law of the LORD,

And in His law he meditates day and night.

Psalm 1:2

SUGGESTED READING

Conformed to His Image, Revised Edition, chapter 15

THE MIXED LIFE

When evangelicals study Scripture, they typically look more for precepts and principles than for an encounter with God in the depths of their being. The practice of lectio divina *can correct this lack of balance.*

Conformed to His Image, Revised Edition, 177

We recommend your approach to Christian living be one that is "mixed." We suggest a balanced combination of an active approach (which focuses on *doing*) and a contemplative approach (which focuses on *being*). In your pursuit of God, it's possible that your tendencies, habits, or lack of exposure have caused you to miss out on some otherwise beneficial active and contemplative practices for deepening your love of God. Practices at either end of a spectrum aren't necessarily opposed to one another; consider them as invitations to a complementary approach.

For the pairs in table 12, consider:

1. What extreme might result from dwelling on one at the avoidance of the other?
2. What balance occurs when a complementary approach is embraced?

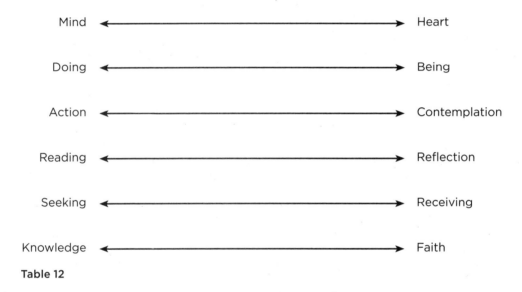

Mind	←————————————→	Heart
Doing	←————————————→	Being
Action	←————————————→	Contemplation
Reading	←————————————→	Reflection
Seeking	←————————————→	Receiving
Knowledge	←————————————→	Faith

Table 12

GUIDED PRACTICE

Use the following guide to practice sacred reading on your own, using Romans 8:1–2.[10]

Note: If you're going through this guide in a group setting, consider taking fifteen to twenty minutes to complete this exercise now, either individually or as a group. Alternatively, participants can complete this exercise on their own before the next group meeting, and you can then review the results together.

Here are some beginning tips.

- Designate a place suitable for sacred reading, preferably away from your normal areas of work.
- Begin with a prayer of preparation, such as Psalm 19:14 or Psalm 119:18.
- Keep in mind, this is not a lockstep, 1-2-3-4 process. Prayer can occur at any time.

Lectio Guide

LECTIO DIVINA PRACTICE EXERCISE #1

Scripture	"There is now no condemnation for those who are in Christ Jesus. For the law of the Spirit of life in Christ Jesus has set you free from the law of sin and of death" (Romans 8:1–2).
Read (*lectio*)	➔ Slowly read the Scripture passage *several times*.
	Tips: • Read aloud to help capture the passage in your memory. • Read prayerfully, asking, "Lord, what are you saying to me in this passage?"
Reflect (*meditatio*)	➔ Reflect and ruminate on the *words and phrases* in the text.
	Tips: • Allow enough time to enjoy the text. • Don't demand immediate gratification or try to control the outcome.
	➔ Which words, phrases, or images speak to you most?
Respond (*oratio*)	➔ Offer the internalized passage back to God in the form of a personalized prayer of adoration, confession, renewal, petition, intercession, affirmation, or thanksgiving.
	Tips: • When you get distracted, return to your selected word(s) or phrase(s). • Be receptive as the Lord speaks to you.
Rest (*contemplatio*)	➔ What word or image encapsulates the spirit of the passage for you?
	➔ Take a few minutes to present yourself before God in silence and yieldedness. When your mind wanders, center yourself by returning to the spirit of the passage.
	Tips: • The frustration of apparent failure is common; don't let it stop you. • Consider reducing your exposure to media and other forms of distraction to enhance your capacity for contemplation.

Table 13

LECTIO REVIEW AND MORE PRACTICE

Answer the following questions after completing your *lectio divina* exercise on Romans 8:1–2.

- Was there an aspect of this exercise that you found challenging?

- Was there an aspect of this exercise that you found rewarding?

- Was there an aspect of this exercise that you found surprising?

Use the guide on the next page to complete an additional *lectio* practice with a passage of your choice, or try one of these options: Deuteronomy 6:4–6; Psalm 46:10–11; Jeremiah 17:7–8; John 15:15–17; Colossians 1:15–16; 1 Peter 2:9–10.

LECTIO DIVINA **PRACTICE EXERCISE #2**

Scripture	
Read (*lectio*)	➔ Slowly read the Scripture passage *several times.*
	Tips: • Read aloud to help capture the passage in your memory. • Read prayerfully, asking, "Lord, what are you saying to me in this passage?"
Reflect (*meditatio*)	➔ Reflect and ruminate on the *words and phrases* in the text.
	Tips: • Allow enough time to enjoy the text. • Don't demand immediate gratification or try to control the outcome.
	➔ Which words, phrases, or images speak to you most?
Respond (*oratio*)	➔ Offer the internalized passage back to God in the form of a personalized prayer of adoration, confession, renewal, petition, intercession, affirmation, or thanksgiving.
	Tips: • When you get distracted, return to your selected word(s) or phrase(s). • Be receptive as the Lord speaks to you.
Rest (*contemplatio*)	➔ What word or image encapsulates the spirit of the passage for you?
	➔ Take a few minutes to present yourself before God in silence and yieldedness. When your mind wanders, center yourself by returning to the spirit of the passage.
	Tips: • The frustration of apparent failure is common; don't let it stop you. • Consider reducing your exposure to media and other forms of distraction to enhance your ability for contemplation.

Table 14

Devotional Spirituality

GROWING IN LOVE WITH GOD

KEY VERSE

He got up and came to his father. But while he was still a long way off, his father saw him and felt compassion for him, and ran and embraced him and kissed him.

Luke 15:20

SUGGESTED READING

Conformed to His Image, Revised Edition, chapter 16

LEARNING FROM THE PRODIGAL

Read Luke 15:11–32, making observations of the main characters' actions and attitudes.

	Oldest Son	Youngest Son	Father
Actions			
Attitudes			

Table 15

➤ Is there an attitude in this story that you identify with most easily?

➤ Which is the hardest attitude for you to adopt?

➤ What do the actions and attitude of the father in the parable reveal about God's actions and attitude?

THE WAY OF RENUNCIATION

Without renunciation, the gifts of God will take the place of God, and our relationship with him will consist more of wanting things from him rather than wanting him alone.
Conformed to His Image, Revised Edition, 190

➤ Make a list of gifts that God has given you. Make sure to consider tangible, spiritual, and relational blessings.

• Tangible blessings

• Spiritual blessings

• Relational blessings

PRAY: Pray through your list of gifts, considering the following elements of prayer.

- *Adoration.* Offer praise to God, acknowledging his goodness, grace, and generosity.
- *Confession.* Confess and ask God for forgiveness if you have cherished the gift more than the Giver.
- *Renewal.* Ask God to renew your mind with the truth of James 1:17, that "every good thing given and every perfect gift is from above, coming down from the Father of lights, with whom there is no variation or shifting shadow."
- *Petition.* Ask God to turn your heart toward him as you enjoy and exercise these gifts.
- *Intercession.* Ask God to show you how you may use his gifts to serve another.
- *Thanksgiving.* Thank God for his gifts and his love toward you.

YOUR SOURCE OF LIFE AND LOVE

The source of our life and love is Christ, who reveals that abiding in him is the key to flourishing. Our communion with him aids us against spiritual enemies. Nonetheless, those enemies come, and we must be prepared.

> *We all experience a natural inertia, a downward pull, an entropy of relational energy that deteriorates our communion with God and with others. Unless we are vigilant, the flame of our initial love for Christ can quietly diminish, and even the embers can grow cold. But if we are faithful to the practice of meditating on the glory of God and the beauty of Jesus, we will love him by beholding him.*
>
> Conformed to His Image, Revised Edition, 193

Enemies of Spiritual Devotion

Using the following list of enemies of spiritual devotion, discuss with a trusted spiritual mentor or friend (or with a discipleship group) how these areas are currently affecting your passion for Christ. How might these enemies creep in if you don't guard against them?

- Unresolved disobedience

- Complacency

- Erosion in spiritual disciplines

- External obedience (conformity to rules for rules' sake)

- Love of truth more than Jesus

- Elevation of service and ministry above Jesus

- Greater commitment to institutions than to Jesus

Cultivating Passion

Read John 15:1–11 and answer the following questions.

- What are the results of a branch that abides in the vine?

- Trace the connections among the following concepts found in this passage: *love, abiding, obedience,* and *joy.*

- What causes the production of fruit in this metaphor, and how does this answer apply to your growth in Christ?

- Now review the list of enemies of spiritual devotion. How does the imagery of the vine and the branches help you guard against the enemies on that list?

O my soul, above all things and in all things always rest in the Lord, for he is the eternal rest of the saints.

Grant me most sweet and loving Jesus, to rest in You.

Thomas à Kempis, *The Imitation of Christ*

PRAY: The beginning of this prayer from Thomas à Kempis focuses on resting in Jesus. Consider the parallel between the concepts of resting and abiding. Then, adapt the final line of his prayer into your own prayer to God.

Holistic Spirituality

THE CENTRALITY OF CHRIST

KEY VERSE

The LORD gives wisdom;
From His mouth come knowledge and understanding.

Proverbs 2:6

SUGGESTED READING
Conformed to His Image, Revised Edition, chapter 17

AVOIDING COMPARTMENTALIZATION

It is a common tendency to separate our lives into various components such as family, work, and finances. However, holistic spirituality recognizes that Christ is central to our lives and not a mere component.

➤ Make a list of ten areas of importance to your schedule, whether categories (school, work, family, ministry, finances, social activity) or individual activities (reading books, specific hobbies, physical exercise, prayer).

MY TEN AREAS:

1.
2.
3.
4.
5.
6.
7.
8.
9.
10.

➤ Now envision these ten items in terms of two models (as mentioned in the video):

- Ten separate circles representing important areas of your life (the compartmentalized model)
- Ten spokes radiating from the hub, which is Christ (the holistic model)

➤ How does the second approach affect the following areas?

- Your sense of peace

- Your sense of purpose

- Your sense of gratitude

➤ How does a holistic approach to life free you from a legalistic approach, in which you attempt to fill your ledger with the "right" balance of "spiritual" items?

➤ In what way(s) does a holistic approach increase your sensitivity to evangelistic opportunities?

➤ How does a holistic approach help you prioritize life's activities?

➤ In what way does a holistic approach infuse meaning into all of your tasks, even the mundane ones?

The seventeenth-century poet George Herbert captured the holistic approach in his poem "The Elixir," which celebrates doing everything for the sake of Christ and celebrates the dignity which that brings to all actions, even something as mundane as sweeping a room. Consider memorizing this poem or one or two of its stanzas.

THE ELIXIR

Teach me, my God and King,
In all things Thee to see,
And what I do in anything
To do it as for Thee.

Not rudely, as a beast,
To run into an action;
But still to make Thee prepossest,[11]
And give it his perfection.

A man that looks on glass,
On it may stay his eye;
Or if he pleaseth, through it pass,
And then the heav'n espy.

All may of Thee partake:
Nothing can be so mean,[12]
Which with his tincture—"for Thy sake"—
Will not grow bright and clean.

A servant with this clause
Makes drudgery divine:
Who sweeps a room as for Thy laws,
Makes that and th' action fine.

This is the famous stone
That turneth all to gold;
For that which God doth touch and own
Cannot for less be told.

                              George Herbert

HOLISTIC HAPPINESS

Because you were designed to seek the happiness found only in God, you will inevitably flit restlessly from one false pursuit to the next if you don't embrace a holistic outlook. Conforming to the image of Christ happens in the context of everyday life. But you will have to stop long enough to examine life's questions through a holistic and long-term lens. Instead we're often given to:

- Avoidance
- Diversion
- Entertainment
- Escape

➤ Consider these four categories of distractions. To which are you most inclined?

➤ What motivating factor drives you toward this lesser option?

➤ Short-term pleasures aren't necessarily wrong, but good things can distract us from the best thing (Christ). How can you call this truth to the forefront of your mind next time you're prone to distraction?

There's a scene in the film *Don Quixote* in which Quixote tells Sancho Panza about the look in the eyes of soldiers who lay dying in his arms—a look which seemed to be asking a question. "Was it the question, 'Why am I dying?'" asks Sancho. "No," replies Quixote, "it was the question, 'Why was I living?'"

➤ Consider again that list of distractions. Are these things for which you want to live?

Happiness is attainable, but not through the world's methods. Instead, it requires true wisdom, which will ultimately point to Christ. Read the following passage from Proverbs 3, and then answer the questions that follow.

> How blessed is the man who finds wisdom
> And the man who gains understanding.
> For her profit is better than the profit of silver
> And her gain better than fine gold.
> She is more precious than jewels;
> And nothing you desire compares with her.
> Long life is in her right hand;
> In her left hand are riches and honor.
> Her ways are pleasant ways

And all her paths are peace.
She is a tree of life to those who take hold of her,
And happy are all who hold her fast.

Proverbs 3:13–18

- What is the key to finding happiness according to these verses?

- What are the other attainable desires mentioned in the passage? (Mark these in some way.)

- How does the world's recommended methods of pursuing happiness contrast with the passage?

- How does holistic pursuit of Christ offer hope for attaining happiness?
  (Use 1 Corinthians 1:30 along with the Proverbs 3 passage to inform your answer.)

SKILL IN THE ART OF LIVING WELL

> *Wisdom is skill in the art of living life with each area under the dominion of God. It is the ability to use the best means at the best time to accomplish the best ends.*
>
> *Conformed to His Image, Revised Edition, 209*

➤ The understanding of wisdom communicated in this quote is not shared by the world. Look at James 3:13–17 and contrast the two types of wisdom presented in the passage.

TWO TYPES OF WISDOM

Wisdom from Above	Wisdom Not from Above

Table 16

PRAY: Consider James 1:5, which also talks about wisdom. Let this verse be a timely reminder of your simple responsibility to access the gracious generosity of God. Use the verse to pray now for wisdom from God.

➤ Proverbs 2:1–6 describes a holistic approach to wisdom. Write down the verbs from this passage. Let them be prompts for pursuing wisdom in the midst of your routines.

➤ You explored the relationship between wisdom and the fear of the Lord in session 11. How does the fear of the Lord motivate you to pursue a holistic spirituality?

Holistic Spirituality

AN INTEGRATED LIFE

KEY VERSE

Whether, then, you eat or drink or whatever you do, do all to the glory of God.

1 Corinthians 10:31

SUGGESTED READING

Conformed to His Image, Revised Edition, chapter 18

THE SPIRITUAL/SECULAR DIVORCE

The disparity between 11:00 on Sunday morning and 11:00 on Monday morning can be enormous.

Conformed to His Image. Revised Edition, 220

An integrated life means doing all things for the glory of God, rather than compartmentalizing life into "sacred" and "secular" spheres.

➤ Failing to view life as an integrated whole and instead adopting a compartmentalized view can lead to disparities between belief and behavior. Why is this the case?

➤ Considering your life as a whole, list five qualities you want to exhibit (such as generosity) and five practices you want to make part of your routine (such as weekly rest).

Five Desired Qualities	Five Desired Habits

Table 17

➤ How many of these qualities and habits can be instantaneously gained?

➤ What current priorities, pursuits, or habits are preventing you from acquiring the items on your list?

PRAY: Small degrees of faithfulness or infidelity can shape our lives over the long run. Pray through the list you wrote, asking God for the strength of will to pursue these items through his empowering presence.

➤ How does an integrated approach to life (with Christ as the center) make these goals more achievable than does a compartmentalized mindset?

➤ You won't wake up tomorrow to find yourself suddenly spiritual. Instead, it takes small, intentional steps each day to work toward your goals. What one thing will you commit to do starting immediately (or as soon as it is feasible) in order to move toward your goal in the power of Christ?

EVERYTHING MATTERS

You probably noticed the repeated statement "everything matters" in the video session. This phrase communicates an important truth reflected in holistic spirituality: even the garbage can be for glory.

EXERCISE:[13] Brother Lawrence, a Frenchman who lived in a monastery in the seventeenth century, committed to doing "little things for the love of God, who regards not the greatness of the work, but the love with which it is performed." We can do the same, committing the most mundane acts of our lives to the Lord. Choose one of the following ordinary tasks, or come up with your own. Each time you start that activity, say to yourself (even if you think it sounds funny), "I'm going to do this in Jesus' name," and then give thanks to him as you do it.

Activity I'll do in Jesus' name, thanking him:

☐ Getting the mail
☐ Taking out the trash
☐ Doing the dishes
☐ Cooking or eating dinner (or another meal)
☐ Picking up your kid(s) from school
☐ Other (an ordinary chore, errand, or activity that you do with regularity):

_____

Incarnational Living

The world of commerce, art, education, politics, family, sorrow, pleasure, science and sociology; all is insignificant compared with the infinitely rich reality of God, yet all things are significant . . . because of the Incarnation.

Martin Thornton, *Christian Proficiency*

Incarnational living means recognizing the spiritual significance in every situation. You can enhance this recognition by cultivating the skill of praying short, internal prayers in the midst of day-to-day activities. Consider the ways in which you might pray:

- Pray for someone while having a conversation with them.
- Pray, expressing gratitude to God, while paying your bills.
- Pray while preparing or eating a meal.
- Pray while getting dressed, asking God to clothe you spiritually as well.
- Pray at work while moving between tasks or interacting with coworkers.
- Pray for the person to whom you're sending an email or text (you could even email or text the prayer).[14]

Losing Focus

The manner and habits of prayer in the previous list can combat your temptation to lose focus and slip back into compartmentalized living. For each of the following temptations, consider how the manner and habits of prayer can keep you from reverting to sacred-secular divisions. Write your thoughts in the space provided.

- The allure of materialism

- Believing that your desires for what is your best good are superior to God's design

- Lack of spiritual passion

- Desire for honor in the sight of others

CHRIST, PREEMINENT

Figure 4 represents the facets of a Christ-centered, integrated life. Notice the vertical relationship between God and self (top and bottom quadrants) and the horizontal relationships with others (left and right quadrants).

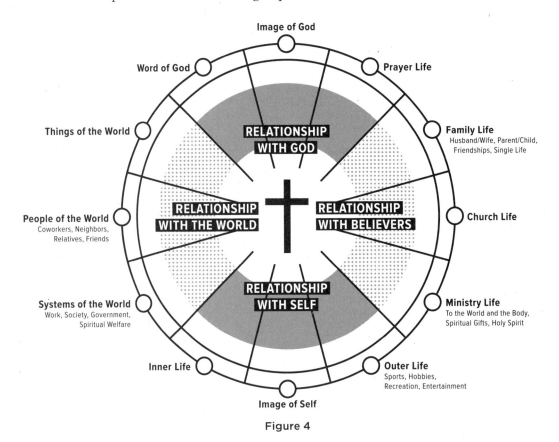

Figure 4

➤ Considering the visual of the spiritual life shown in figure 4, are there any areas in which you've not let Christ be preeminent?

EXERCISE: Consider taking one of the twelve sections each month for the next year. Focus on that relationship area. Then, by this time next year, you will have taken great steps toward living an integrated life. You may want to journal about your results each month. Organize these results according to how you see:

- God glorified
- Yourself satisfied
- Others evangelized and edified

Holistic Spirituality

RELATIONSHIPS, WORK, AND SOCIETY

KEY VERSES

Do all things without grumbling or disputing; so that you will prove yourselves to be blameless and innocent, children of God above reproach in the midst of a crooked and perverse generation, among whom you appear as lights in the world, holding fast the word of life, so that in the day of Christ I will have reason to glory because I did not run in vain nor toil in vain.

Philippians 2:14–16

SUGGESTED READING

Conformed to His Image, Revised Edition, chapter 19

RELATIONSHIPS

Our relationships are crucial to our spiritual formation and to our witness to a watching world. Because of this, we must learn how to integrate faith and practice in these areas.

Husband-Wife

Note: Even if you're not married or don't have children, this material can be helpful for the purpose of encouraging other families in the body of Christ. It's also helpful to review these truths in light of living in a society that often promotes unbiblical alternative ideals.

The Lord God fashioned into a woman the rib which He had taken from the man, and brought her to the man. The man said,

> "This is now bone of my bones,
> And flesh of my flesh;
> She shall be called Woman,
> Because she was taken out of Man."

For this reason a man shall leave his father and his mother, and be joined to his wife; and they shall become one flesh. And the man and his wife were both naked and were not ashamed.

Genesis 2:22-25

Identify the following principles from Genesis 2:22–25.

- Role of God in marriage

- Principle of individuality

- Principle of unity

- Principle of diversity

- Principle of respect

- Principle of intimacy

- Principle of growth

- Principle for families

➢ Marriage, even Christian marriage, is difficult. Thinking through the principles you just identified, consider how success or failure in any of these areas contributes to marital unity or discord, respectively.

PRAY: If you are married, discuss and pray through these principles with your spouse. If you are not married, pray through these areas with a focus on how you can prepare to be a loving spouse, or on how you can support and encourage these principles in others' marriages.

➢ How does the holistic spirituality goal of having Christ as the preeminent source of worth and pleasure free you to be a better spouse?

> The greatest enemy to marriage is the selfish attitude that is concerned with the other person's character and one's own needs. Other-centered love focuses on our own character and the other person's needs.
>
> *Conformed to His Image, Revised Edition,* 240

While the foregoing quote reads nicely, these words are hard to put into practice! If you're married, it may help to have a calendar meeting with your spouse in which you ask for your spouse's needs for the week. Resist the urge to share your needs unless asked. In private, write in your calendar your spouse's needs and the area of your character that you will be working on. Pray for both your spouse and your own growth in character throughout the week.

Married couples often struggle with consistency or intimacy in the following areas. Consider these areas with your spouse and talk with each other about how you can draw closer to God in them.

- Praying and reading Scripture
- Conversation
- Sex

Parent-Child

Just as holding Christ preeminent gives us the freedom to be better spouses, it also gives us the freedom to be better parents.

➤ How does Christ's preeminence influence the way you should view and treat your children? (Treat this question hypothetically if you do not have children.)

➤ Parents—not the state or even the church—hold the primary role of providing for their children's needs. For the following areas, first make each an item of prayer. Then assess how well you're doing in each category. Finally, discuss these items with your spouse or even your child, if appropriate, and make a plan for improving and growing in the Lord. (If you don't have children, think of a family with children who could use your prayers on their behalf.)

- Material needs

- Spiritual instruction

- Psychological well-being

- Intellectual pursuit

- Emotional stability

- Physical health and growth

➤ You can't impart what you don't possess. Look again at the six areas you just reviewed. How well are you doing in each area for yourself? What will you do to ensure you're on a path to growth in Christ in each area?

PRAY: Although you can do your best to shape your children and model strong, Christlike character for them, their relationship with God is ultimately *theirs* and thus out of your hands. Surrender your children to God now, and pray that their relationships with him would be strong.

Friendships

Look up the following verses and identify the actions of a good friend. Use this list as a guide for being a good friend and for choosing good friends.

Proverbs 17:9   _____

Proverbs 17:17   _____

Proverbs 18:19   _____

Proverbs 18:24   _____

Proverbs 27:6   _____

Proverbs 27:9   _____

Proverbs 27:17   _____

Ecclesiastes 4:9–10   _____

Romans 12:15   _____

Hebrews 3:13   _____

➤ Which of these actions do you find hardest to do for others?

PRAY: Loneliness is a difficult path to walk, but it can also be a season of growth. Ask God to sustain you if you're in such a season, and that he would send a friend at the right time. Pray that this friend would exhibit the actions from the list you created, and pray that you would be that sort of friend.

WORK

Holistic spirituality involves approaching work through a new lens—seeking to serve God rather than ourselves in it (see Matthew 6:24).

➢ For many, work becomes the center of the circle, replacing Christ. Why is it easy to succumb to this temptation?

➢ What are some ways to combat this temptation?

➢ How does a proper perspective on work help us do the following?

- Reflect the image of God

- Serve others

- Give generously

- Worship

- Express gratitude

➢ What is the proper attitude of a Christian community toward work? (See 1 Thessalonians 4:11–12 and 2 Thessalonians 3:10–15.)

God has created us to both work and rest, with a healthy balance of each (see Genesis 2:15 and Mark 2:27, for example). When we overwork and ignore the principle of rest, it may reveal areas of sin. When tempted to overwork, ask yourself whether this is evidence of the following:

• Greed

• Lack of trust

• Mismanagement of time

• Failure to prioritize

• Arrogance

SOCIETY

> *Our focus of ministry should be shaped by the calling and burden God gives us. We must beware of the common mistake of universalizing our ministry passion. Otherwise we will take on a moralistic attitude and assume that our calling should be obligatory for others.*
>
> *Conformed to His Image, Revised Edition, 249*

We can become each other's enemies instead of fellow workers if we fail to recognize the varied nature of problems and needs in society as well as the varied giftings and provisions of God for his body (the church) to address those problems and needs.

➤ Is there a societal issue that you're more passionate about than most other people are?

➤ Are you serving in this area of passion in a way that functions alongside other ministries of the church?

➤ What danger is there in a passionate and godly calling that is pursued with a compartmentalized rather than holistic approach?

➤ What universal practice for all believers do you see prescribed in Philippians 2:14–15? What benefit is this practice to both yourself and those around you—believers and unbelievers?

Do all things without grumbling or disputing; so that you will prove yourselves to be blameless and innocent, children of God above reproach in the midst of a crooked and perverse generation, among whom you appear as lights in the world.

Philippians 2:14–15

➤ How does this description of believers in Philippians affect your understanding or expectations of the society in which we live?

➤ It's easy to give up on society, but doing so fails to recognize the God-ordained purpose for the lives of every member of society. How does Acts 17:26–27 offer encouragement against cynicism?

EXERCISE: Prayerfully consider establishing or deepening a personal connection with a person or a group in need. Serving widows, visiting prisoners, ministering to the elderly, doing volunteer work in your profession, or participating in a ministry that assists the poor with food, clothing, and housing are all ways of loving and serving people in the name of Jesus (Matthew 25:34–40).

➤ Read the following excerpt from C. S. Lewis's *The Screwtape Letters*, in which the senior devil Screwtape counsels the junior devil Wormwood. How does your understanding of the holistic approach to spirituality help combat the unbalance presented in this fictitious yet perceptive account of a Christian's interaction in society?

About the general connection between Christianity and politics, our position is more delicate. Certainly we do not want men to allow their Christianity to flow over into their political life, for the establishment of anything like a really just society would be a major disaster. On the other hand, we do want, and want very much, to make men treat Christianity as a means; preferably, of course, as a means to their own advancement, but, failing that, as a means to anything—even to social justice. The thing to do is to get a man at first to value social justice as a thing which the Enemy demands, and then work him on to the stage at which he values Christianity because it may produce social justice.

C. S. Lewis, *The Screwtape Letters*

Holistic Spirituality

STEWARDSHIP AND PURPOSE

KEY VERSES

Let a man regard us in this manner, as servants of Christ and stewards of the mysteries of God. In this case, moreover, it is required of stewards that one be found trustworthy.

1 Corinthians 4:1–2

SUGGESTED READING

Conformed to His Image, Revised Edition, chapter 20

STEWARDSHIP

The following quote summarizes holistic spirituality.

Holistic spirituality involves a growing responsiveness to the lordship of Christ in every internal and external aspect of our lives. It is not a question of developing a list of theoretical priorities (e.g., God first, family second, work and ministry third) but a matter of allowing the centrality of Christ to determine and empower what we should do in each day. Seen this way, Christ is our life and Lord in all our activities, and whatever we are doing at the moment becomes our priority focus.

Conformed to His Image, Revised Edition, 252

> ➤ Given this summary, what advantage(s) does the holistic approach have for one who is a steward of another's possessions?

> ➤ Once you have realized that you are a steward, how does the holistic approach help in evaluating and carrying out your life purpose?

The Steward Mindset

> ➤ Below, make a list of your most treasured possessions. Include tangible items, but also list intangible items (such as relationships, giftings, opportunities, and experiences).

MY LIST OF POSSESSIONS:

> ➤ Now review your list with the following two primary thoughts of a steward in mind. What impact do these two thoughts have on your list?

1. You own nothing.

2. You are not here on earth on your own business.

➢ How does this steward mindset relate to our first lessons in relational spirituality (sessions 2–4), in which we discussed loving God completely, loving ourselves correctly, and loving others compassionately?

➢ What do the following conversations between Jesus and his apostles reveal about the character of our Master? Are they what you would expect of a master (boss, owner, person in authority over you)?

> He who has My commandments and keeps them is the one who loves Me; and he who loves Me will be loved by My Father, and I will love him and will disclose Myself to him.
>
> John 14:21

> No longer do I call you slaves, for the slave does not know what his master is doing; but I have called you friends, for all things that I have heard from My Father I have made known to you.
>
> John 15:15

The great question at the center of biblical stewardship is whether you are lord of your life or Christ is. Look at table 18 contrasting the great *I will* with the great *Thy will*. We face a decision between these wills many times in a day.

PRAY: Ask God to help you choose his will over your own in your upcoming decisions.

THE BATTLE OF WILLS

I Will	Thy Will
"You said in your heart, 'I will ascend to heaven; I will raise my throne above the stars of God, And I will sit on the mount of assembly In the recesses of the north. 'I will ascend above the heights of the clouds; I will make myself like the Most High.'" (Isaiah 14:13-14)	"Your kingdom come. Your will be done, On earth as it is in heaven." (Matthew 6:10) He was saying, "Abba! Father! All things are possible for You; remove this cup from Me; yet not what I will, but what You will." (Mark 14:36)

Table 18

FIVE AREAS OF STEWARDSHIP

There are five basic areas of stewardship. In addition to the usual areas of time, talent, and treasure, we also include truth and relationships.

Stewardship of Time

"I didn't have enough time" is an excuse we've all made. When you use this excuse, what does it convey about how you see the following?

- The wisdom of our Master

- Awareness of your surroundings

- Your wisdom

The following passages reveal key principles related to stewarding time. Review each passage, listing any principle it reveals.

- Psalm 31:14–15   _____
- Psalm 90:12   _____
- Romans 13:11–12   _____
- 2 Corinthians 4:18 _____
- Ephesians 5:15–16 _____

Stewardship of Talent

Our talent and giftings don't belong to us but to the One who gave them to us. The following verses reveal key principles when it comes to stewarding talent. Review each verse, listing any principle it reveals.

- Romans 12:6   _____
- 1 Corinthians 4:7   _____
- 1 Peter 4:10   _____

PRAY: We'll explore talent and giftings further in session 26, "Spirit-Filled Spirituality: The Gifts of the Spirit." For now, pray that God will give you the wisdom to recognize your talents and to surrender them to the purposes of your Maker.

Stewardship of Treasure

The Bible mentions money or material possessions more than 2,300 times.

- What does this emphasis tell you about the importance of the topic?

- What does this emphasis tell you about our nature and inclinations as humans? Do you struggle with stewardship of treasure?

- What impact—positive and negative—does your stewardship of treasure have on the other areas of stewardship?

  Time

  Talent

Truth

Relationships

The following passages reveal key principles when it comes to stewarding treasure. Review each passage, listing any principle it reveals.

- Deuteronomy 8:17–18 _____
- Job 1:1–3   _____
- Psalm 24:1   _____
- Psalm 50:10–11   _____
- Matthew 6:19–21   _____
- 1 Timothy 6:6–10   _____
- 1 John 3:17   _____

> *If we can get straight on the principle of 100 percent ownership, we will be ready for the principle of 100 percent stewardship.*
>
> *Conformed to His Image, Revised Edition*, 256

Stewardship of Truth

This area is usually not thought of in terms of stewardship. Look at Luke 8:18, which, taken out of context, appears to be another verse about treasure but is actually about stewardship of truth.

> Take care how you listen; for whoever has, to him more shall be given; and whoever does not have, even what he thinks he has shall be taken away from him.
>
> Luke 8:18

The following questions guide you in understanding the link between Jesus' instruction to "take care how you listen" and the parables he told.

➤ Read the parables in Luke 8:4–15. What do these parables tell you about the subject matter? (Hint: What does the seed represent in the parable of the sower [v. 11], and how does the command in the parable of the lamp [v. 18] relate to it?)

➤ What is the "more" that shall be given? (Hint: What is given by the sower [v. 5], and what is given by the lamp [v. 16]?)

➤ What does "whoever has" mean in this verse? (See vv. 15–16.)

➤ Why does Jesus say, "So take care how you listen"?

The following passages reveal key principles when it comes to stewarding truth. Review each passage, listing any principle it reveals.

- Matthew 12:36   _____
- John 8:31–32   _____
- Ephesians 6:17   _____
- 2 Timothy 3:16–17 _____

- James 1:18–22 _____
- James 3:1 _____

Stewardship of Relationships

> The resources of time, talent, and treasure that the Lord has entrusted to us are never ends in themselves. The wise steward learns to leverage these temporal resources into eternal good, and this is accomplished by learning and living the Word of God and by investing our lives in people.
>
> *Conformed to His Image, Revised Edition, 256*

The following passages reveal key principles related to stewarding relationships. Review each passage, listing any principle it reveals.

- Job 42:10 _____
- Luke 16:9 _____
- Colossians 4:5 _____
- 3 John 5–8 _____

➤ How might these principles help you steward your current relationships?

PURPOSE

> Holistic spirituality distinguishes our primary calling in life—knowing and loving God—from our secondary calling—expressing this relationship in everything we do and with everyone we encounter. If the secondary purpose is not related to the primary, we dichotomize the spiritual and the secular when they should be integrated. When this happens, our relationship with the Lord is disconnected from the activities of our lives.
>
> *Conformed to His Image, Revised Edition, 257*

All believers have three global purposes, as discussed within the relational spirituality facet:

1. Love God completely
2. Love self correctly
3. Love others compassionately

These purposes are manifested in your life through various roles (husband, daughter, neighbor, writer) and opportunities.

PRAY: Prayerfully reflect on your global purposes as well as your role purposes. Then consider what specific goals and objectives would assist you in fulfilling these purposes for your life. You may want to let Philippians 3:8–11 guide you.

Process Spirituality

PROCESS VERSUS PRODUCT

KEY VERSE

Do not worry about tomorrow; for tomorrow will care for itself. Each day has enough trouble of its own.

Matthew 6:34

SUGGESTED READING

Conformed to His Image, Revised Edition, chapter 21

LIVING IN THE FUTURE

Your concept of identity, whether it comes from the world or from the Word, will shape your ideas about the future and therefore your actions in the present. Consider the models presented in figure 5.

The first image depicts an approach in which achievement and activity inform who you are. The second depicts an approach in which Christ informs who you are, and in which he is, therefore, the basis for what you do.

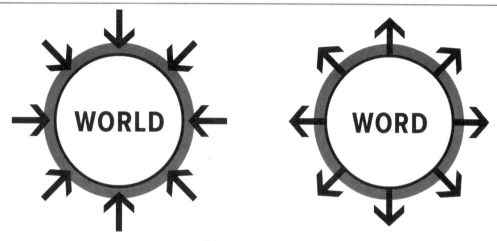

Figure 5

➢ What are the differences in how each approach to defining identity would handle worry?

➢ What are the differences in how each approach would handle setbacks?

➢ What are the differences in how each approach might affect thoughts about establishing one's legacy?

A STEP-BY-STEP JOURNEY

Not every step of a journey is pleasant. The following are likely steps of any person's life journey.

- Uncertainty
- Setbacks
- Disappointment
- Surprise
- Joy

How do the following passages equip you for these steps of this journey?

- Romans 5:3–5

- 2 Corinthians 4:16–18

- Ephesians 2:19–22

- James 1:1–5

- 1 Peter 4:12–16

What do the following passages teach you about comparing your journey to that of others?

- John 21:18–22

- 2 Corinthians 10:12–18

➢ What difficulties might you encounter in embracing the mindset described in the following quote? Do cultural expectations influence your expectation of your own growth process?

> *Our task is to place ourselves under the conditions favorable to growth and look to God for our spiritual formation. He uses different paces and methods with each person. . . . If we fail to accept this uneven developmental process, we will be impatient with God and with ourselves as we wait for the next growth spurt or special infusion of grace.*
>
> *Conformed to His Image, Revised Edition, 269*

➢ How does a mindset of comparison and impatience hinder you in loving others as you love yourself?

➢ Read Hebrews 5:11–14. What does this passage teach about how we ought to grow?

FAITH, HOPE, AND LOVE

Faith, hope, and love characterize our life in Christ. They each speak uniquely to how we view the past (faith in Christ's redemptive work), future (hope in our eternity with Christ), and present (love manifesting the life of Christ). The world may not understand how we can base our present devotion on the past and the future, which are unseen and invisible. A. W. Tozer wrote of the oddity of the Christian's journey:

> He feels supreme love for One whom he has never seen, talks familiarly every day to Someone he cannot see, expects to go to heaven on the virtue of Another, empties himself in order to be full, admits he is wrong so he can be declared right, goes down in order to get up, is strongest when he is weakest, richest when he is poorest and happiest when he feels worst. He dies so he can live, forsakes in order to have, gives away so he can keep, sees the invisible, hears the inaudible and knows that which passeth knowledge.
>
> A. W. Tozer, *The Root of the Righteous*

➤ Identify the elements of faith, hope, and love in Tozer's characterization of the Christian.

Faith

The faith that pleases God involves three components: knowledge, trust, and action. We might quickly identify that second component—trust—but overlook the surrounding components of knowledge and action.

➤ Identify each of these elements in Paul's prayer for the Colossians.

> For this reason also, since the day we heard of it, we have not ceased to pray for you and to ask that you may be filled with the knowledge of His will in all spiritual wisdom and understanding, so that you will walk in a manner worthy of the Lord, to please Him in all respects, bearing fruit in every good work and increasing in the knowledge of God; strengthened with all power, according to His glorious might, for

the attaining of all steadfastness and patience; joyously giving thanks to the Father, who has qualified us to share in the inheritance of the saints in Light.

Colossians 1:9–12

➤ Ponder the following two statements, and then write out your thoughts on the nature of faith.

The heart cannot rejoice in what the mind rejects.

Biblical faith is not a leap into the dark but a step into the light.

If you find yourself in a season of dryness, consider how a study in apologetics resources may bolster your faith through increased confidence in newly attained or newly refreshed knowledge.

➤ God has created us with varying dispositions. Some of us may tend toward knowledge, others toward trust, and others toward action. Do you find yourself drawn to one of these more than to the others? Why is that, do you think?

➤ Is there an area in which you classify yourself as weak? An area that you tend to avoid?

➤ How might you embrace strengthening that area as part of your spiritual growth process?

PRAY: Make 2 Thessalonians 2:15–17 a source of prayer for strength in knowledge, trust, and action.

> Stand firm and hold to the traditions which you were taught, whether by word of mouth or by letter from us.
>   Now may our Lord Jesus Christ Himself and God our Father, who has loved us and given us eternal comfort and good hope by grace, comfort and strengthen your hearts in every good work and word.
>
> 2 Thessalonians 2:15–17

Hope

Process spirituality focuses on your being alive to the present moment, yet hope points toward something in the future. That hope for the future influences the process of your growth in the present.

How does biblical hope for the future affect the following?

• Your present attitude

• Your present ambitions

• Your present actions

➤ Read Hebrews 6:17–19. How does hope bring together past, present, and future?

> In the same way God, desiring even more to show to the heirs of the promise the unchangeableness of His purpose, interposed with an oath, so that by two unchangeable things in which it is impossible for God to lie, we who have taken refuge would have strong encouragement to take hold of the *hope* set before us. This *hope* we have as an anchor of the soul, a *hope* both sure and steadfast and one which enters within the veil.
>
> Hebrews 6:17–19, emphases added

Love

Of faith, hope, and love, Paul writes, "the greatest of these is love" (1 Corinthians 13:13). One reason love is the greatest virtue is because it is the application in the present of our faith in things past and our hope in things future.

For an encouraging example of believers who lived out this application, consider the Thessalonians. In his letter to them, Paul gives thanks for their example of growing and living in faith, hope, and love:

> We give thanks to God always for all of you, making mention of you in our prayers; constantly bearing in mind your work of faith and labor of love and steadfastness of hope in our Lord Jesus Christ in the presence of our God and Father.
>
> 1 Thessalonians 1:2-3

➤ Meditate on and write down the implications of living out this verse in your life.

➤ Don't overlook Paul's mention of the "presence of our God and Father." In what way is God's presence helpful in the metaphor of the spiritual life as a journey?

➤ Popular concepts of love are often passive and emotional. For example, we say that someone "falls in love" or that love is a feeling that occurs in response to a person. How does Paul's description of love differ from passive, emotional concepts?

PRAY: Let 1 Thessalonians 1:2–3 inspire your prayers. Pray that you too will:

1. Work in faith
2. Labor in love
3. Remain steadfast in hope

Process Spirituality

BEING VERSUS DOING

KEY VERSE

The Lord answered and said to her, "Martha, Martha, you are worried and bothered about so many things."

Luke 10:41

SUGGESTED READING

Conformed to His Image, Revised Edition, chapter 22

THE PROBLEM OF BUSYNESS

Rampant busyness can blur any semblance of borders between the various aspects of our daily lives. Many of us stuff our schedules full of activities and neglect to rest. This often leaves us exhausted and empty, not having had the time to be filled spiritually. If you find yourself in this situation, it may help to think about busyness as it pertains to five categories of your life: home, work, recreation, ministry, and your walk with God.

Busyness in Your Home

➤ Do an inventory of activities such as television, computer time, or your children's lessons, sports, and clubs. Is there an area that you can and should pare?

➤ As increasing numbers of people work remotely, how can you guard against your home being unrecognizable from your office?

➤ Read Deuteronomy 6:5–9. How well does your current home structure line up with the instructions there?

➤ Is there a formal time that you need to create to address those issues?

➤ Do you need to create room for more spontaneous times with your family?

➤ Is your home a place that allows for you and your family to flourish spiritually and welcomes others in the name of the Lord?

Busyness in Your Work

Consider the following assessment, written in 1972:

Most middle-class Americans tend to worship their work, to work at their play, and to play at their worship. As a result, their meanings and values are distorted. Their relationships disintegrate faster than they can keep them in repair and their lifestyles resemble a cast of characters in search of a plot.

Gordon Dahl, *Work, Play, and Worship in a Leisure-Oriented Society*

➤ Assess whether your work allows quality time for the following:

• Personal spiritual formation

• Family

• Involvement with a church

• Leisure

If not, you're working too long and too hard. While there are days when your work may require more of your time and effort, you should not be in hard-push mode all the time. If you are, it's likely that you've come to root your identity in your work.

➤ Earlier sessions spoke of a search for security, significance, and satisfaction. Consider whether your busyness in work serves as a substitute for Christ in any of the four areas.

➤ In what ways is rest from work a challenge to your faith?

Busyness in Your Recreation

Failure to plan for recreation may result in one of two extremes: (1) never stopping to rest, or (2) shirking responsibility.

EXERCISE: Consider your calendar for the next month. Pick a weekend (or weekday, if your schedule allows it) and plan for leisure, whether that's rest with no agenda or an outing to a sporting event, a concert, or an outdoor activity. Afterward, consider how this activity shaped the week leading up to the planned recreation and how it shaped the week after your time of recreation.

Busyness in Your Church Work or Ministry

Not every request is a need or calling from God, even if that request is for ministry. These questions may help you decide whether to say yes to a ministry request.

• Are you involved in multiple ministries? List them here.

• In some of those ministries, is there someone else in your church who could perform the task as well or better?

- Is there someone in your church whom you could disciple to minister alongside you and then replace you?

- Does the ministry help you to know God better?

- Does the ministry prevent you from honoring commitments to your spouse or children?

- Can you do the work without grumbling or complaining?

Busyness in Your Walk with God

It may seem odd to say our walk with God can grow too busy. But if we take an outside-in approach to our spiritual life, trying to meet the requirements of a mental checklist, it can rob us of intimacy with God and move us toward controlling the direction of our walk.

➤ What do the following verses teach about our walk with God?

- Mark 1:32–39

- Luke 5:15–16

CAUSES VERSUS CHRIST

External action should derive from internal reality, and this requires a rhythm of solitude and engagement, restoration and application, intimacy with Christ and activity in the world.

Conformed to His Image, Revised Edition, 281

Causes can be admirable, but they also may detract from our pursuit of Christ. This is partially because it is easier to quantify the results associated with a cause than it is to measure growth of intimacy with Christ.

BEING AND DOING: GETTING THE ORDER RIGHT

Being	Doing
Intimacy with Christ	Activity in the world
Solitude	Engagement
Abiding	Serving
Interior	Exterior
Relational calling	Dominion calling
Calling	Character
Invisible	Visible
Real life	Reflected life
Restoration of spiritual energy	Application of spiritual energy
Perspective	Practice
Rest	Work

Table 19

➤ Both columns in table 19 represent necessary areas of life—being and doing. However, if we get the order wrong and place *doing* before *being*, the result can be perfectionism and legalism. Go through each row of the table. Consider what happens to the item in the *being* column if the item in the *doing* column is sought first.

➢ Look anew at the greatest commandment. What do you notice about the order of words?

> You shall love the Lord your God with all your heart, and with all your soul, and with all your mind, and with all your strength.
>
> Mark 12:30

PRACTICING GOD'S PRESENCE[15]

Finding times of peace and seclusion is important to your prayer life. An additional skill to develop is learning to pray even in the midst of everyday living. The latter type of prayer is called recollection, and it can be either habitual or actual.

> Habitual recollection *is analogous to a man's or a woman's love for a spouse or children and does not require an ongoing consciousness. Just as we can form a habitual identity as being a husband, a wife, or a parent, so we can ask for the grace to form a habitual state of mind as a follower of Jesus Christ.* Actual recollection *involves turning to God at regular times throughout the day.*
>
> *Conformed to His Image, Revised Edition,* 285

EXERCISE: The process imagery used in Scripture can aid in this recollection. Look through the following images that describe the ongoing process of life in God's presence. Choose one you resonate with. Write it out on an index card and keep it with you to read throughout the day. Meditate on phrases that stand out, and ask God to help you live it out or obey it.

- Abide in Jesus (John 15:4–7).
- Set your mind on the things of the Spirit (Romans 8:5–6).
- Walk by the Spirit (Galatians 5:16, 25).
- Keep seeking the things above, where Christ is (Colossians 3:1–2).
- Rejoice always (1 Thessalonians 5:16).
- Pray without ceasing (1 Thessalonians 5:17).
- Give thanks in everything (1 Thessalonians 5:18).
- Run with endurance the race set before you, fixing your eyes on Jesus (Hebrews 12:1–2).

Process Spirituality

TRUST, GRATITUDE, AND CONTENTMENT

KEY VERSES

Search me, O God, and know my heart;

Try me and know my anxious thoughts;

And see if there be any hurtful way in me,

And lead me in the everlasting way.

Psalm 139:23-24

SUGGESTED READING

Conformed to His Image, Revised Edition, chapter 23

TRUST

Trust is key to our relationship with God. Without it, we give in to one of the great enemies of growth in Christ: the craving for control over our environment and the results of our actions. When we do trust God, we experience the relief of knowing that God not only has our best interests at heart but also has the power to bring them about.

"Without God we cannot; without us he will not." This quote (often attributed to Augustine) is packed with implications regarding our relationship with God.

➤ What does this quote say about the following?

- Grace

- Sovereignty

- Freedom

- Dependence

- Power

- Responsibility

- Ability

- Qualification

- Strength

- Weakness

- Possibility

- Limitation

- Cooperation

- Control

- Desire

- Duty

- Trust

- Training

Our role within life's opportunities and outcomes is illustrated in table 20.

OPPORTUNITY, OBEDIENCE, AND OUTCOME: OUR ROLE VERSUS GOD'S ROLE

Opportunity	Obedience	Outcome
Divine sovereignty	Human responsibility	Divine sovereignty

Table 20

Our tendency is to branch out from obedience and occupy all three territories. To do so is to fail to obey and to disrupt the entire process.

➤ Is there an area of your life in which you're struggling to obey God?

PRAY: This need to trust and obey, without worrying about the outcome, was captured well by Blaise Pascal, and we would all do well to pray along these lines:

O Lord, I know only one thing, and that is that it is good to follow You and wicked to offend You. Beyond this, I do not know what is good for me, whether health or sickness, riches or poverty, or anything else in this world. This knowledge surpasses both the wisdom of men and of angels. It lies hidden in the secrets of Your providence, which I adore, and will not dare to pry open.

Blaise Pascal, *Pensées*

➤ Read the following passages. How does each encourage obedience over trying to control and manipulate opportunities and outcomes?

- 2 Samuel 7:1–17

- Mark 4:26–29

- Acts 16:5–10

- 1 Corinthians 3:5–11

You do not have the capacity to measure your ministry. Here's the full quote from the novel *Middlemarch,* mentioned in this video session, about the impact of the character Dorothea Brooke:

> The effect of her being on those around her was incalculably diffusive: for the growing good of the world is partly dependent on unhistoric acts; and that things are not so ill with you and me as they might have been is half owing to the number who lived faithfully a hidden life, and rest in unvisited tombs.
>
> George Eliot, *Middlemarch*

➤ It may be grace that prevents us from understanding the impact of our service in the Lord. What negative result might occur if you knew and could measure every ministry success in your life?

PRAY: Thank God for his sovereignty and for his grace despite your lack of full obedience.

GRATITUDE

The great mistake regarding gratitude is to wait for it to happen. Spiritual formation that values spontaneity over discipline is likely no further along than when it started. Gratitude is a choice—a habit to cultivate—rather than a feeling (though it may be accompanied by a feeling).

➤ How will you, this week, cultivate gratitude in the following ways?

- Daily

- Intentionally

➤ Read Hosea 13:6. What does cultivating a heart of gratitude prevent?

➤ Use table 21 to record a personal history of God's goodness and grace to you.

MY PERSONAL HISTORY OF GOD'S GOODNESS AND GRACE

God's Deliverance in the Past

God's Benefits in the Present

God's Promises for the Future

Table 21

In cultivating gratitude, do not overlook the seemingly insignificant items. Every moment is an opportunity for practicing God's presence. Be inspired by G. K. Chesterton's attitude toward acknowledging God in the present.

> You say grace before meals. All right. But I say grace before the play and the opera, and grace before the concert and pantomime, and grace before I open a book, and grace before sketching, painting, swimming, fencing, boxing, walking, playing, dancing; and grace before I dip the pen in the ink.
>
> G. K. Chesterton

➤ Having read this quote, what are some "smaller" areas in which you can give thanks?

CONTENTMENT

Like trust and gratitude, contentment involves a choice of focus: will you set your heart on what you do have or what you don't have?

EXERCISE: Consider the following statements, based on Paul's words in Philippians 3:8–11. Make them "flash prayers" (short, silent prayers, uttered anywhere) throughout your day. Consider writing them on cards or sticky notes that you place on your desk or mirror.

- "I count all things as loss for the surpassing value of knowing you, Jesus."
- "May I gain Christ."
- "I want to be found in Jesus."
- "I have God's righteousness."
- "I know God and Christ's resurrection power."
- "I fellowship in Christ's sufferings."

Contentment belongs to those who let Christ determine the content of their lives. Review figure 6, noticing the progression of self-centered content versus that of Christ-centered content. Note too the horizontal contrast of the two paths.

➤ Are there area(s) under the "Self" column in which you struggle?

WHO DETERMINES THE CONTENT OF YOUR LIFE?

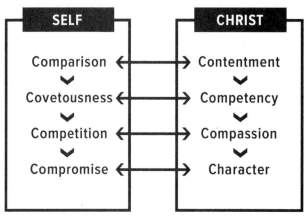

Figure 6

PRAY: For any struggle area(s), use the contrasting word in the "Christ" column to guide your prayer for forgiveness and healing.

> *As we learn the secret of contentment, we will be less impressed by numbers, less driven to achieve, less hurried, and more alive to the grace of the present moment.*
>
> *Conformed to His Image, Revised Edition, 299*

Spirit-Filled Spirituality

WALKING IN THE POWER OF THE SPIRIT

KEY VERSE

Walk by the Spirit, and you will not carry out the desire of the flesh.

Galatians 5:16

SUGGESTED READING

Conformed to His Image, Revised Edition, chapter 24

RESPONDING TO THE SPIRIT

The Holy Spirit has long been the Cinderella of the Trinity. The other two sisters may have gone to the theological ball; the Holy Spirit got left behind every time. But not now.

Alister McGrath, *Christian Theology: An Introduction*

➤ In session 14, you considered the importance of what comes into your mind when you think about God. Does the Holy Spirit come to mind when you're thinking about God? Whether he does or doesn't, why might you have that tendency?

➤ Your reaction to Spirit-filled spirituality (or maybe even the term "Spirit-filled" itself) may be overly influenced by your perception of those who have differing views and practices regarding the Holy Spirit. Privately assess, or discuss with your group, how your religious upbringing and practices (or your observations of others' upbringing and practices) influence your view toward Spirit-filled spirituality.

➤ Your disposition toward Spirit-filled spirituality may fall into an extreme of either rejection or obsession. These errors likely have more to do with your focus on self than with your focus on God.

1. In what way is the error of rejection me-centered rather than God-centered?

2. In what way is the error of obsession me-centered rather than God-centered?

➤ Read Galatians 5:16–25, in which we're reminded that we "live by the Spirit" (v. 25), should "walk by the Spirit" (v. 16), and should "keep in step with the Spirit" (v. 25 NIV). According to your reading, how is your life potentially affected by wrong views of the person and work of the Holy Spirit?

THE PERSON AND WORK OF THE HOLY SPIRIT

The Trinity Revealed

While people may differ on the role and manifestations of the Spirit, views that the Spirit is something less than personal and less than God are problematic to a proper understanding of God's nature.

➤ What do the following verses teach you about the triune God?

- Matthew 3:16–17

- Acts 5:3–4

- Romans 8:2–17

- Titus 3:4–8

Inward and Outward Filling

The Scriptures describe both the inward and outward work of the Holy Spirit. You can gain insight into these manifestations by tracing the usage through two words referencing the Spirit's filling: *plērēs/plēroō* and *pimplēmi*.

Use table 22 to record your findings on the filling of the Spirit as you trace these words through the New Testament. Use these questions to guide your study:

- What do you observe as you compare and contrast their usage?
- Are there different focuses for the two words?
- What do the manifestations of the Spirit produce?
- What can be said about the nature of the filling, judging by the word used?

FILLING OF THE SPIRIT IN THE NEW TESTAMENT: A WORD STUDY

Terms	
plērēs (πληρης) / *plēroō* (πληροω)	*pimplēmi* (πιμπλημι)
References	
Luke 4:1 Acts 6:3, 5; 7:55; 11:24; 13:52 Ephesians 5:18	Luke 1:41, 67 Acts 2:4; 4:8, 31; 13:9
Observations and Thoughts	

Table 22

KNOWING, BEING, AND DOING

A full-orbed spirituality involves grounding in biblical truth and sound doctrine (knowing), growing in character and personal experience with God (being), and developing gifts and skills in the service of others (doing).

Conformed to His Image, Revised Edition, 313, emphases added

Examine the following list of a dozen ministries of the Holy Spirit, mentioned in this video session. How do these Spirit ministries relate to knowing, being, and doing? Scriptures are provided as an aid, but your answers may go beyond what is in the verses.

1. Convicting (John 16:8–11)

2. Regenerating (Titus 3:5–6)

3. Baptizing (1 Corinthians 12:13)

4. Sealing (Ephesians 1:13–14)

5. Indwelling (Romans 8:9)

6. Filling (Ephesians 5:18)

7. Empowering (Ephesians 3:16)

8. Assuring (1 John 3:24)

9. Illuminating (1 Corinthians 2:10–16)

10. Teaching (John 16:13–16)

11. Praying (Romans 8:26–27)

12. Gifting (1 Corinthians 12:4–11)

PRAY: Ask God for discernment about your tendencies in the area of Spirit-filled spirituality and for balance in your thinking, affections, and actions.

Spirit-Filled Spirituality

THE GIFTS OF THE SPIRIT

KEY VERSES

There are varieties of gifts, but the same Spirit. And there are varieties of ministries, and the same Lord. There are varieties of effects, but the same God who works all things in all persons.

1 Corinthians 12:4-6

SUGGESTED READING

Conformed to His Image, Revised Edition, chapter 25

UNITY AND DIVERSITY

Here's a breakdown of the phrasing in this session's key verses:

varieties of gifts	the *same* Spirit
varieties of ministries	the *same* Lord
varieties of effects	the *same* God who works all things in all persons

Table 23

➤ How does 1 Corinthians 12:4–6 enhance your view of the Trinity?

➤ In what ways are unity and diversity on display in the gifts of the Spirit?

Table 24 highlights the gifts mentioned in the video, although the list may not be exhaustive. For each variety of *gift*, consider what *ministry* may flow from that gifting and what *effects* it may have in the lives of individuals and in the church as a whole.

GIFTS OF THE SPIRIT AND THEIR EFFECTS

Gifts	Ministries	Effects
Prophecy Romans 12:6; 1 Corinthians 12:10, 28-29; 14:1-40; Ephesians 4:11		
Service Romans 12:7		
Teaching Romans 12:7; 1 Corinthians 12:28-29; Ephesians 4:11		
Exhortation Romans 12:8		
Giving Romans 12:8		
Leadership Romans 12:8		
Mercy Romans 12:8		

Table 24   *(cont.)*

Wisdom		
1 Corinthians 12:8		
Knowledge		
1 Corinthians 12:8		
Faith		
1 Corinthians 12:9		
Healing		
1 Corinthians 12:9, 28, 30		
Miracles		
1 Corinthians 12:10, 28, 29		
Distinguishing of spirits		
1 Corinthians 12:10		
Tongues		
1 Corinthians 12:10, 28, 30; 14:1-30		
Interpretation of tongues		
1 Corinthians 12:10, 30; 14:5, 13, 26-28		
Apostleship		
1 Corinthians 12:28, 29; Ephesians 4:11		
Helps		
1 Corinthians 12:28		
Administration		
1 Corinthians 12:28		
Evangelism		
Ephesians 4:11		
Shepherding or pastoring		
Ephesians 4:11		

Table 24

DISCOVERING GIFTS

➤ How do the following three prerequisites affect your ability to discover and exercise spiritual gifts?

1. Receiving the gift of salvation in Christ

2. Walking in fellowship with the Lord

3. Desiring to develop your gifts

➤ Write down your spiritual gift(s) as best you can discern (it may or may not be in table 24 in the previous section). If you're not sure what your gift(s) are, consider asking a spiritual mentor or friend for insight into your gift(s).

MY GIFT(S):

GUARDING GIFTS

Reflecting on the gift(s) God has given you, review the following potential abuses of spiritual gifts. Consider areas in which you are susceptible to or guilty of abuse. Ask God for forgiveness and strength to grow in this gift. Discuss and pray with a fellow member of Christ's body through this list.

• Seeking your benefit above the benefit of others

- Seeking gifts by merit

- Exercising your gift in the power of the flesh

- Apathy toward discovering and using your gift

- Jealousy and/or discouragement over the distribution or development of gifts

- Pride over the gift you've received

- Seeking the gift as an end in itself

- Holding extreme positions about gifts that are not warranted by Scripture

- Allowing your gift to be counterfeited through the flesh or the devil

- Projecting your gift onto others

He gave some as apostles, and some as prophets, and some as evangelists, and some as pastors and teachers, for the equipping of the saints for the work of service, to the building up of the body of Christ; until we all attain to the unity of the faith, and of the knowledge of the Son of God, to a mature man, to the measure of the stature which belongs to the fullness of Christ.

Ephesians 4:11–13

Spirit-Filled Spirituality

OPENNESS AND DISCERNMENT: A BALANCE

KEY VERSES

Desire earnestly to prophesy, and do not forbid to speak in tongues. But all things must be done properly and in an orderly manner.

1 Corinthians 14:39–40

SUGGESTED READING

Conformed to His Image, Revised Edition, chapter 26

PROPER DESIRE

It is better to practice spiritual discernment while welcoming the work of the Spirit. It is healthy not only to keep the windows open but also to keep the screens on.

Conformed to His Image, Revised Edition, 332

➤ When considering the Holy Spirit's presence in your life, are you more likely to proceed with cautious discernment or to seek his encounter with unquestioning openness?

➤ Given your tendency, how might you "desire earnestly" yet act "properly and in an orderly manner" (as this session's key verses put it)?

➤ What harm can come from desiring earnestly without acting in a proper and orderly manner?

➤ What harm can come from valuing order above manifestations of the Spirit?

PROPER FOCUS

Consider these words of Jesus regarding the Holy Spirit:

> When He, the Spirit of truth, comes, He will guide you into all the truth; for He will not speak on His own initiative, but whatever He hears, He will speak; and He will disclose to you what is to come. He will glorify Me, for He will take of Mine and will disclose it to you. All things that the Father has are Mine; therefore I said that He takes of Mine and will disclose it to you.
>
> John 16:13–15

- What actions does the Spirit perform, according to these verses?

- What do these verses teach you about discerning whether manifestations of the Spirit in a believer's life are in accordance with proper actions (as you listed in the previous question)?

- According to these observations, how should your desires line up with the Spirit's actions and relationship within the Trinity?

PRAY: Offer thanks to God that he has given his Spirit to his followers. Then pray that he would increase your discernment regarding spiritual manifestations in addition to your openness to the Spirit's work in your life.

POWER THROUGH PURITY

One of the ways in which we can prepare our hearts for openness to the Spirit is through confessing our disobedience. Often we have:

- Sloppy thought-lives
- Flabby wills
- Anemic passions and aspirations

➢ From this list, identify an area that you should make a matter of prayer this week.

➤ How does disobedience in the three aforementioned areas relate to what Christ called the foremost commandment (Mark 12:30)?

➤ How does disobedience in these areas affect your ability to carry out the second great commandment (Mark 12:31)?

EXERCISE: One habit we can cultivate is, upon first waking in the morning, to dedicate the day to trusting the Father, abiding in the Son, and walking by the Spirit. The card shown in figure 7 is designed to help you embrace this routine.[16] Try this exercise every morning for a week and see if it enhances your discernment and openness to the Spirit's work during your day.

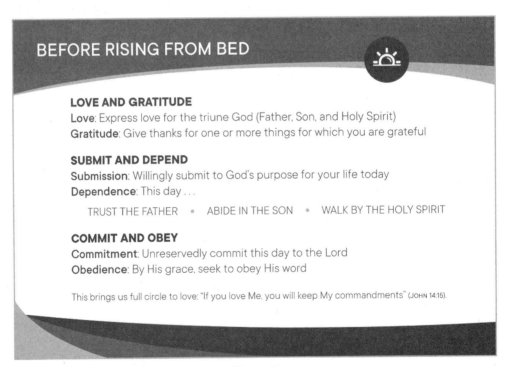

BEFORE RISING FROM BED

LOVE AND GRATITUDE
Love: Express love for the triune God (Father, Son, and Holy Spirit)
Gratitude: Give thanks for one or more things for which you are grateful

SUBMIT AND DEPEND
Submission: Willingly submit to God's purpose for your life today
Dependence: This day . . .

TRUST THE FATHER   •   ABIDE IN THE SON   •   WALK BY THE HOLY SPIRIT

COMMIT AND OBEY
Commitment: Unreservedly commit this day to the Lord
Obedience: By His grace, seek to obey His word

This brings us full circle to love: "If you love Me, you will keep My commandments" (JOHN 14:15).

Figure 7

Warfare Spirituality

WARFARE WITH THE FLESH AND THE WORLD

KEY VERSES

You were dead in your trespasses and sins, in which you formerly walked according to the course of this world, according to the prince of the power of the air, of the spirit that is now working in the sons of disobedience. Among them we too all formerly lived in the lusts of our flesh, indulging the desires of the flesh and of the mind, and were by nature children of wrath, even as the rest.

Ephesians 2:1–3

SUGGESTED READING

Conformed to His Image, Revised Edition, chapter 27

THE REALITY OF WARFARE

Both Spirit-filled spirituality and warfare spirituality are good tests for what this video session referred to as "text management," a selective reading of the Scriptures that avoids areas of discomfort or what we may consider to be fringe or overplayed subjects. Warfare spirituality focuses on the dynamics of the multifront spiritual battle or conflict every follower of Christ is in.

➤ Consider this description of warfare spirituality as well as the discussion of this facet in the video session. What is your disposition toward warfare spirituality? How aware are you of it as it pertains to your life?

➤ Consider how your approach to spiritual warfare may be influenced by the following filters.

- Theological filters (theological positions that inform your understanding of how the spiritual realm is manifested in the physical realm)

- Emotional filters (personal predispositions regarding spirit beings and their activity)

- Cultural filters (societal influences that affect whether you accept or reject certain realities about the spiritual realm)

➤ A survey across both Old and New Testaments gives insight into the nature of spiritual warfare. What do the following passages reveal about the reality, scope, and effect of spiritual warfare?

- Leviticus 17:7

- Deuteronomy 32:16–17

- 1 Samuel 16:13–15

- Psalm 106:37

- Matthew 8:16

- Ephesians 6:12

- Revelation 12:7–9

➤ In 1 John 3:8, we're told that "the Son of God appeared for this purpose, to destroy the works of the devil." How does this truth affect your view of spiritual warfare?

WARFARE WITH THE FLESH

➤ The term "flesh" (σάρξ, *sarx*) has several uses in Scripture. Look up the following references and record how the word is used in each context. (You will want to consult different Bible translations as each will translate the term differently.)

- John 1:14

- Romans 1:3–4

- Romans 7:5, 14

- 1 Corinthians 15:39

- Ephesians 6:5

- Philippians 3:3–4

- Hebrews 9:10

This last exercise reveals how the term "flesh" may be used to denote the (physical) body. However, the term also may be used to connote sinful inclination. The manifestations of the flesh, in the sinful sense of the word, are outlined in Galatians 5:19–21.

- Make a list of the fleshly manifestations named in the passage.

- Do you notice any categories or groupings of sin?

- The fruit of the Spirit (as opposed to the manifestations of the flesh) appears in the verses immediately following (Galatians 5:22–23). How does the fruit of the Spirit combat the manifestations of the flesh? Write specific examples in the space provided.

Our chief identity is now in Christ, who has defeated the flesh (Galatians 2:24). Although we do not find our identity in our past or present sins, each of us has a different flesh signature that we should be aware of.

➤ What fleshly thoughts, choices, or habits are you prone to? (You may also want to consult other lists that use the terminology "old man" or "old self" instead of "flesh": Ephesians 4:22–31; Colossians 3:2–9.)

Though we walk in the flesh, we do not war according to the flesh.

2 Corinthians 10:3

➤ Two great principles of spiritual warfare are given to us in 2 Corinthians 10:3. Record them here.

1.
2.

➤ In this verse, Paul writes that we walk in the flesh, yet in Romans 8:4, he writes that we do *not* walk in the flesh. How does your study on the word "flesh" (σάρξ, *sarx*) help you understand why Paul isn't contradicting himself?

➤ What are some specific ways you can put these two principles into practice with respect to your fleshly inclinations?

WARFARE WITH THE WORLD

➤ As with the term "flesh," so too the term "world" (κόσμος, *kosmos*) has multiple uses, as you can see in these verses. Record the usage beside each reference.

- Matthew 16:26   _____
- Mark 16:15   _____
- John 3:16   _____
- John 17:5   _____
- 1 Corinthians 4:9   _____
- 1 Corinthians 5:10   _____

➤ What is the relationship between the flesh and the world? Use the following verses (each of which mentions the flesh and the world together) to formulate your answer.

- 2 Corinthians 1:12

- James 4:1–5

- 1 John 2:15–16

➤ Paul's letter to the Philippians is instructive in its characterization of the world and how we navigate through it as believers. As you read this passage, mark the actions and attitudes that will help you prevail in this life.

Just as you have always obeyed, not as in my presence only, but now much more in my absence, work out your salvation with fear and trembling; for it is God who is at work in you, both to will and to work for His good pleasure.

Do all things without grumbling or disputing; so that you will prove yourselves to be blameless and innocent, children of God above reproach in the midst of a crooked and perverse generation, among whom you appear as lights in the world, holding fast the word of life, so that in the day of Christ I will have reason to glory because I did not run in vain nor toil in vain. But even if I am being poured out as a drink offering upon the sacrifice and service of your faith, I rejoice and share my joy with you all. You too, I urge you, rejoice in the same way and share your joy with me.

Philippians 2:12-18

Warfare Spirituality

WARFARE WITH THE DEVIL AND HIS ANGELS

KEY VERSE

Submit therefore to God. Resist the devil and he will flee from you.

James 4:7

SUGGESTED READING

Conformed to His Image, Revised Edition, chapter 28

THE NATURE AND WORK OF SATAN

➤ Satan appears on the scene early in both Testaments of Scripture. Read these four chapters: Genesis 3, Job 1–2, and Matthew 4. Then answer the following questions to better understand the enemy's tactics as well as your own vulnerability and ability to withstand temptation in God's power.

- What is the context of the temptation in each of these passages? What events immediately precede Satan's attack?

(continued writing space)

- What descriptors are given regarding the state or actions of those being attacked?

- What descriptors of Satan are given in these chapters?

- What role does the Word of God play in the unfolding of events?

- Do you see any common battle tactics that Satan employs?

- What do you observe about God's actions in these stories?

THE NATURE AND WORK OF DEMONS

Fascination and fear are common responses to the idea of demons. Let's look to Scripture's teaching in order to subdue both far-fetched speculation and inordinate worry about demons.

➤ According to the following passages, in what areas do demons seek to influence and oppress?

- Mark 9:17–18

- Acts 5:3

- 1 Corinthians 10:20

- 1 Timothy 4:1

- James 3:14–15

- Revelation 16:14

The duty of soldiers in war is to obey their commander. In spiritual warfare, the greatest commandment of our Commander is to love him with heart, mind, soul, and strength. These four areas are also the ones our enemy attacks.

➤ In the verses you just explored, note any references to these areas of heart, mind, soul, and strength. In what way does the activity of demons speak against this greatest commandment?

Doubt about the existence of a malign focus of evil is to be found, by and large, only in Christian lands. . . . It would be broadly true to say that disbelief in the devil is a characteristic only of materialistic Western Christendom.

Michael Green, *I Believe in Satan's Downfall*

➤ The attribution of activities to demons is more prevalent in the Global South and other parts of Asia than in America. Why do you think that is the case?

THE ENEMY'S OBJECTIVE AND END

➢ We know little about the origin of Satan and demons; the when, where, and why of their fall; and their ultimate goal. Why, do you think, does God not reveal more to us about these subjects?

➢ Scripture does reveal *some* objectives of Satan and his demons. What do you observe about those objectives in the following verses?

- Luke 22:31

- 2 Corinthians 4:3–4

- 1 Peter 5:8

- Revelation 20:7–8

➢ While we may not know Satan's ultimate goal, we do know his ultimate destiny. Use the following passages as sources of comfort for the battle.

- Romans 8:37–39
- 1 Corinthians 15:50–57
- Hebrews 2:14–15
- Revelation 20:1–10

Further Reading

Literature abounds on the subject of demons and spiritual warfare, although much of this material is untrustworthy. If you're interested in reading more on the subject, here's a suggested list.

- *Three Crucial Questions about Spiritual Warfare* (Clinton E. Arnold)
- *Sense and Nonsense about Angels and Demons* (Kenneth D. Boa and Robert M. Bowman Jr.)
- *Angels and the New Spirituality* (Duane Garrett)
- *Angels: God's Secret Agents* (Billy Graham)
- *The Gospel According to Angels* (Robert W. Graves)
- *Encyclopedia of Angels* (Rosemary Ellen Guiley)
- *Angels (and Demons): What Do We Really Know about Them?* (Peter Kreeft)
- *The Screwtape Letters* (C. S. Lewis)
- *Demon Possession* (John Warwick Montgomery, ed.)
- *Powers of Evil* (Sydney H. T. Page)
- *Angels among Us* (Ron Rhodes)

Warfare Spirituality

THE WEAPONS OF OUR WARFARE

KEY VERSES

Though we walk in the flesh, we do not war according to the flesh, for the weapons of our warfare are not of the flesh, but divinely powerful for the destruction of fortresses.

2 Corinthians 10:3-4

SUGGESTED READING

Conformed to His Image, Revised Edition, chapter 29

A WINNABLE WAR

Our Hope

Dark forces can manipulate the physical world along with the minds and wills of some people. When we consider the unrelenting and cruel attacks from these forces—targeting even children—the battle against the enemy may seem hopeless. However, Scripture assures us this is not the case.

➤ What promises of victory do the following verses confirm?

- Romans 12:21

- James 4:7

- Galatians 1:3–4

- Ephesians 6:10–11

- 1 John 2:13–14

- 1 John 5:4–5

➤ A serious pursuit of growth in Jesus involves spiritual warfare. Even after reading Scripture's promises of victory, does the idea of being a target of the enemy still invoke fear in you?

PRAY: Prayerfully meditate (or do a *lectio* exercise, as discussed in session 16) on this reassuring promise:

> You are from God, little children, and have overcome them; because greater is He who is in you than he who is in the world.
>
> 1 John 4:4

➤ Record your thoughts and reflections on this verse in the space provided.

Our Help

➤ The spiritual forces of the enemy are not the only group arrayed for battle. What do you learn about angelic forces and the army of God from the following verses?

• 2 Kings 6:15–17

• Psalm 103:19–21

• Hebrews 1:14

• Hebrews 12:22–24

• Revelation 5:11

➢ Considering these verses, write a summary statement of the help available to us in spiritual warfare.

THE NEED FOR PREPARATION

Discipline and Dependence

> *We need to be prepared for sudden skirmishes by wielding the spiritual weapons God has provided for our victory. This requires discipline and dependence.*
>
> Conformed to His Image, Revised Edition, 372

➢ According to the following passages, what are the disciplined tasks specifically required for spiritual warfare? After you compile this list, reflect on which practices to add to your routine.

- Matthew 17:21

- Luke 9:23

- Romans 6:13

- Romans 12:1–2

- Romans 13:11–14

- Galatians 5:25

- Colossians 3:8–9

- Hebrews 12:11

- 1 Peter 1:13–15

The Armor of God

Be strong in the Lord and in the strength of His might. Put on the full armor of God, so that you will be able to stand firm against the schemes of the devil. For our struggle is not against flesh and blood, but against the rulers, against the powers, against the world forces of this darkness, against the spiritual forces of wickedness in the heavenly places. Therefore, take up the full armor of God, so that you will be able to resist in the evil day, and having done everything, to stand firm. Stand firm therefore, having girded your loins with truth, and having put on the breastplate of righteousness, and having shod your feet with the preparation of the gospel of peace; in addition to all, taking up the shield of faith with which you will be able to extinguish all the flaming arrows of the evil one. And take the helmet of salvation, and the sword of the Spirit, which is the word of God. With all prayer and petition pray at all times in the Spirit, and with this in view, be on the alert with all perseverance and petition for all the saints.

Ephesians 6:10-18

Let's look at the components of armor mentioned in Ephesians 6:10–18. List what each can help protect against (for example, the belt of truth protects against falsehood), and then consider the question and supporting verses that accompany each armor component, to encourage you to grow in knowledge of and confidence with these weapons.

The Belt of Truth

- Protects against:

- What is the significance of putting on this component first?

Supporting verse: 2 Corinthians 10:5

The Breastplate of Righteousness

- Protects against:

- How does the teaching of Ephesians on the heart (1:18; 3:13, 17; 4:18, 32; 5:19; 6:5–6, 22) help you understand the significance of protecting it?

Supporting verse: 2 Timothy 2:22

The Sandals of Peace

- Protect against:

- How is it possible that the equipment that stabilizes a soldier in *battle* is peace?

Supporting verses: Romans 12:18; 14:19

The Shield of Faith

- Protects against:

- If you don't take up the shield of faith, what effect does that have on those in the battle with you?

Supporting verses: James 1:2–4

The Helmet of Salvation

- Protects against:

- How do the truths in Ephesians (2:3; 4:17, 23) relate to the helmet of salvation?

Supporting verses: Romans 12:2; Philippians 4:8; 1 Peter 1:13

The Sword of the Spirit

- Protects against:

- What use is a sword if the one to whom it is given never trains with it? What will you do to train with this weapon?

Supporting verses: Luke 4:4, 8, 12

Ever-Present Prayer and Petition

- Protects against:

- What role does communication play in a battle plan and on the battlefield?

Supporting verses: Matthew 26:38–46

RENEW, RECKON, RESIST

Review and then use the affirmations in figure 8 in the morning or any time of the day to help you in the spiritual battle. Note the three Rs of renew, reckon, and resist—one for each of the three fronts of the warfare.[17]

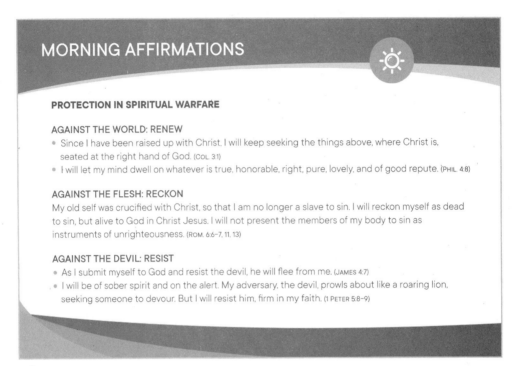

MORNING AFFIRMATIONS

PROTECTION IN SPIRITUAL WARFARE

AGAINST THE WORLD: RENEW
- Since I have been raised up with Christ, I will keep seeking the things above, where Christ is, seated at the right hand of God. (COL. 3:1)
- I will let my mind dwell on whatever is true, honorable, right, pure, lovely, and of good repute. (PHIL. 4:8)

AGAINST THE FLESH: RECKON
My old self was crucified with Christ, so that I am no longer a slave to sin. I will reckon myself as dead to sin, but alive to God in Christ Jesus. I will not present the members of my body to sin as instruments of unrighteousness. (ROM. 6:6–7, 11, 13)

AGAINST THE DEVIL: RESIST
- As I submit myself to God and resist the devil, he will flee from me. (JAMES 4:7)
- I will be of sober spirit and on the alert. My adversary, the devil, prowls about like a roaring lion, seeking someone to devour. But I will resist him, firm in my faith. (1 PETER 5:8–9)

Figure 8

Nurturing Spirituality

A PHILOSOPHY OF DISCIPLESHIP

KEY VERSE

He was saying to them all, "If anyone wishes to come after Me, he must deny himself, and take up his cross daily and follow Me."

Luke 9:23

SUGGESTED READING

Conformed to His Image, Revised Edition, chapter 30

SELF-ASSESSMENT

We cannot follow Jesus when we are asking him to follow us. We limit our spiritual development when we fail to make the transition from seeing Jesus as a problem solver to seeing him as our life.

Conformed to His Image, Revised Edition, 390

Becoming a disciple of Jesus while helping others in that same journey requires commitment to perform certain actions, all of which hold Jesus as their object. The purpose of each of these actions is to lead us closer to Jesus.

➢ Write after the following verses the action required of a disciple.

- Matthew 11:28–29

- Luke 9:23

- John 14:1

- John 14:15, 21

- John 15:4

➢ Of those actions you just listed, which is hardest for you? Why?

➢ If you're not engaged in that action, how does it affect your ability to be a successful disciple? What is the result in the life of others?

The children of God are all at different stages of growth. Progression through stages may be dependent on time and experience. It's also the case that the children of God aren't all equally obedient or thriving. Some may regress through disobedience and fail to abide in Christ. Though still a child of God, they are not fruitful disciples. Consider three stages:

1. Believer (the initial and eternal state of all of God's children)
2. Responding and growing (the ongoing state of those who abide in Christ and his Word)
3. Reproducing disciple (the mature state of the abiding disciple who bears fruit)

➤ Which of these stages are you currently in?

➤ What's the highest stage you've been in during your spiritual walk? How will you progress toward being a reproducing disciple, or how will you continue to progress in that status?

➤ How is each progressive stage dependent on its preceding stage? What does that tell you about the importance of whatever stage you're in?

Hebrews 5:11–14 contrasts what happens when our spiritual growth stagnates and when it thrives. Read the verses, and then answer the questions that follow regarding the expectations and responsibilities of Christ's disciples.

> Concerning him we have much to say, and it is hard to explain, since you have become dull of hearing. For though by this time you ought to be teachers, you have need again for someone to teach you the elementary principles of the oracles of God, and you have come to need milk and not solid food. For everyone who partakes only of milk is not accustomed to the word of righteousness, for he is an infant. But solid food is for the mature, who because of practice have their senses trained to discern good and evil.
>
> Hebrews 5:11-14

➤ What attitude is expressed in this passage toward believers who aren't growing?

➤ What is the result and danger of failing to grow?

➤ What is the result when we are growing as we should?

➤ In 1 Corinthians 11:1, Paul encouraged, "Be imitators of me, just as I also am of Christ." Whether we recognize it or not, our own spiritual growth affects those around us. If you were to ask others to imitate you right now, what would be the result in their lives?

FOCUSING ON OTHERS

➤ According to John 13:34–35, what is the key identifier of a disciple of Jesus?

In this video session, the following definition of love was offered.

LOVE: the steady intention of the will toward another person's highest good

➤ In what ways does this definition differ from worldly definitions of love?

➤ If you're married, in what ways will you progress in discipleship through loving your spouse? If you're not married, how are you channeling your discipleship efforts toward the one or two people you're closest to?

➤ If you're a parent, in what ways will you progress in discipling your children? If you don't have children, how are you engaging in discipleship with those younger in the faith?

➤ As a believer, in what ways will you progress in discipleship by loving fellow church members?

In 2 Timothy, Paul encouraged Timothy, "The things which you have heard from me in the presence of many witnesses, entrust these to faithful men who will be able to teach others also" (2:2).

➤ As you focus on others and disciples multiply, the temptation to move back toward a focus on yourself can come in the form of pride in the number of disciples made. How does the command regarding Timothy's strength in 2 Timothy 2:1 help against such pride?

Better to give a year or so to one or two people who learn what it means to conquer for Christ than to spend a lifetime with a congregation just keeping the program going.

Robert E. Coleman, *The Master Plan of Evangelism*

➤ What do you think of Robert Coleman's assessment? In what way might this be true? In what way might it not be true?

➤ Would your own ministry benefit from focusing on fewer people, but at a deeper level? If so, what changes do you need to make?

Ministry can be difficult as you walk alongside fellow disciples, some of whom will let you down. You may also struggle with assessing the success of your efforts in discipleship and in ministering.

➤ Consider times of ministry when you experienced the most disappointment, discouragement, or disillusionment. How might you use those experiences to encourage someone else's ministry? Write your thoughts:

• Disappointment

• Discouragement

• Disillusionment

PARTNERING WELL

Selfless discipleship allows us to rejoice in the progress of others and to invite others to minister alongside us.

➤ Trace the history of discipleship in the biblical figure of Apollos. What do you learn about discipleship from his story?

- Acts 18:24–19:1

- 1 Corinthians 1:10–13

- 1 Corinthians 3:1–7, 21–23

- 1 Corinthians 16:12

EXERCISE: Acts 15:22 mentions a partnership among four men: Paul, Barnabas, Judas, and Silas. Their ministries were endorsed by the apostles and elders of the early church. It's worth tracing this history to gain insight regarding working with others. A larger study of Acts and the resulting work that followed from the interactions of these men (and those they encounter) is worth your time.

- All four together: Acts 15:30–34
- Paul and Barnabas: Acts 9:22–31; 11:20–30; 12:25–13:7; 13:42–14:20; 15:35–39; Galatians 2:9–13
- Paul and Silas: Acts 15:36–41; 16:19–34; 17:10–16; 18:1–5

Nurturing Spirituality

THE PROCESS, PRODUCT, AND CONTEXT OF DISCIPLESHIP

KEY VERSE

The things you have learned and received and heard and seen in me, practice these things, and the God of peace will be with you.

Philippians 4:9

SUGGESTED READING

Conformed to His Image, Revised Edition, chapter 31

THE PROCESS OF DISCIPLESHIP

Three key components to making disciples are (1) *exposing* people to your own life of discipleship, (2) *equipping* them with truth to apply to their lives, and (3) *encouraging* them toward Christlikeness through your relationship with them. These three components (discussed in the video and summarized here in table 25) are concurrent, not chronological.

THE THREE COMPONENTS OF DISCIPLESHIP

Exposing	Equipping		Encouraging and Exhorting
Example (modeling)	Teaching	Training	Obedience and accountability
	Thinking	Habits	
	Theory	Technique	
	Truth	Skills	
	Principles	Practice	
Being (discipler)	Knowing	Doing	Being (disciple)
Character	Convictions	Conduct	Character
Heart	Head	Hands	Heart

Table 25

Exposing

Last session, you read Paul's charge to the Corinthians: "Be imitators of me" (1 Corinthians 11:1). Similarly, he told the Philippians, "The things you have learned and received and heard and seen in me, practice these things, and the God of peace will be with you" (Philippians 4:9).

➤ Which elements of the discipleship process (exposing, equipping, encouraging) do you see in this verse in Philippians?

➤ What areas of your life would attract potential disciples to Christ? What areas might be a hindrance to them?

➤ Read 1 Peter 3:15. What role does godly character play in your influence of potential disciples? What other elements of being a discipler are present in this verse?

Equipping: Teaching and Training

Teaching Scripture should move beyond the mere delivery of facts. It should also involve training with a view toward encouraging and exhorting disciples to apply truth to their lives. Second Timothy 3:16 is often quoted to stress the inspiration aspect of God's Word, but it points to other qualities of Scripture as well.

➤ What does this verse, along with the subsequent verse (3:17), have to say about Scripture's role in the process of discipleship? (You may want to refer to table 25.)

➤ Examine the two middle columns of table 25. What happens if these pairs are divorced from one another? For example, what is the result of conduct without convictions or of convictions without conduct? Consider each pair.

Encouraging and Exhorting

Teaching and training are not ends in themselves. Ultimately, those being discipled should go on to be disciplers—whom others, in turn, would desire to emulate.

➤ If you're currently involved in teaching and training, how can you gauge the level of character development in those being discipled?

➤ In your teaching and training, what are some specific ways you can provide people with opportunities for obedience and accountability?

➤ Can you think of any areas in which you need to be more obedient and accountable to your own teaching?

You may find it useful to assign sections of *Conformed to His Image* and this study guide as discipleship tools. If you do so, we advise that you allow the user an appropriate amount of time to consider the teaching, practice the training, and prayerfully apply what's been absorbed.

THE PRODUCT OF DISCIPLESHIP

The human disposition to count, control, measure, and manipulate makes us more comfortable with reducing discipleship to a program that creates a quantifiable product. If we overlook this tendency, we will be inclined to define discipleship in terms of outward conformity rather than inward transformation. To do this is to miss the essence of spiritual formation—becoming like the Master by moving from faith in Christ to the faith of Christ.

Conformed to His Image, Revised Edition, 402–3

Discipleship can be hard to gauge, and as we discussed in the previous session, we're all in the process of either progressing or regressing, depending on our faith and obedience to Christ. However, Scripture does offer some measurables for discipleship.

Take the following assessment for yourself; then use it as a tool in your discipleship of others.

- ☐ Am I trusting in Christ alone, apart from any of my works, for my eternal salvation (Ephesians 2:8–9)?
- ☐ Do I walk in good works (Ephesians 2:10)?
- ☐ Do I experience joy (John 15:11)?
- ☐ Do I love fellow believers (John 15:12)?
- ☐ Do I value the Word of God (John 6:68)?
- ☐ Am I a prayerful person (Ephesians 6:18)?
- ☐ Are my activities invested in eternal significance (Romans 13:11–12)?
- ☐ Do I engage and encourage in my local church (Hebrews 10:24–25)?
- ☐ Am I a steward of God's graces (1 Corinthians 4:7)?
- ☐ Am I eager to learn from and serve others (2 Timothy 2:2)?

Consider the following quote from Dallas Willard in light of the checklist you just completed.

Nondiscipleship costs abiding peace, a life penetrated throughout by love, faith that sees everything in the light of God's overriding governance for good, hopefulness that stands firm in the most discouraging of circumstances, power to do what is right and withstand the forces of evil. In short, nondiscipleship costs you exactly that abundance of life Jesus said he came to bring (John 10:10).

Dallas Willard, *The Great Omission*

➤ Making strides toward being more productive disciples is not about assuaging a sense of guilt but about realizing the true "cost of nondiscipleship"—forfeiture of the abundant life God wants for us. What specific changes are you motivated to make?

THE CONTEXT OF DISCIPLESHIP

The mature disciple recognizes that discipleship is not limited to churches or set times of spiritual discovery and practice (as we discussed when we looked at the facet of holistic spirituality). Thus your discipleship context is everywhere. Discipleship should involve both structured pursuits (small group, mentoring, church) and spontaneous, as-you-are-going pursuits (family, professional, societal).

➤ List your spheres of influence, both structured and spontaneous (some may be both). Pray through your list. Ask God to give you wisdom as a discipler and as a disciple in each area. Pray for the people in those spheres. Confess sin in any area. Ask for the grace to continue sensing God's presence and serving people in each area.

Nurturing Spirituality

A PHILOSOPHY OF EVANGELISM

KEY VERSE

How will they preach unless they are sent? Just as it is written, "How beautiful are the feet of those who bring good news of good things!"

Romans 10:15

SUGGESTED READING

Conformed to His Image, Revised Edition, chapter 32

THE SIGNIFICANCE OF EVANGELISM

Evangelism is concerned with the eternal destiny of a person's life. Yet that introduction to the Savior who imparts eternal life is also an invitation to abundant life here and now (John 10:10). Evangelizing is an entry point but not the destination of the discipling process. Understanding that the gospel offers life for the future and the present infuses this earthly sojourn with meaning.

Consider the following quote and the emptiness of a worldview that recognizes a "human problem" with no satisfactory answers for where we are or where we are going.

It is a bit embarrassing to have been concerned with the human problem all one's life and find at the end that one has no more to offer by way of advice than "Try to be a little kinder."

Aldous Huxley

➤ How does the Christian worldview regarding eternity influence how we treat others during our earthly lives?

➤ What would be the ultimate purpose of values such as human kindness if there were no promise of future, eternal life?

➤ How does the Christian understanding of God as transcendent and timeless speak hope to the human condition?

Depending on your unique sojourn, you might not have spent a large portion of your life as an unbeliever. As a result, there may be questions you never wrestled with that would be helpful for you to understand as you share the gospel with others. If you grew up in the church or trusted in Christ for salvation at an early age, the concept of hopelessness, apathy, or even antipathy regarding life may be hard for you to imagine.

➤ Initiate a discussion with a fellow believer who lived part of his or her adult life *without* the good news of Jesus. What was his or her mindset prior to understanding the gospel?

➤ What thoughts did the person have regarding eternity? Meaning? Jesus? The Bible? Christians?

THE PROCESS OF EVANGELISM

➤ Does the prospect of evangelism make you feel uncomfortable? If so, what fears do you have?

➤ How might the concept of evangelism as a process rather than as an event allay your discomfort?

➤ What false assumption lies at the root of a close-the-sale approach (getting someone to make a decision in the moment no matter what) toward evangelism?

➤ Many of the facets we've covered contribute to or deal directly with evangelism. Write out briefly how each of the following facets (see summaries on page 5) relate to the evangelism process? This exercise can help you see how your personal spiritual formation process has an eternal impact in the lives of others.

   • Relational spirituality

- Paradigm spirituality

- Disciplined spirituality

- Motivated spirituality

- Holistic spirituality

- Spirit-filled spirituality

- Warfare spirituality

The focus of evangelism can tend toward the cleverness of the presentation or the passion of the speaker. Philippians 1:15–20 paints a different picture. After reading these verses, answer the following questions.

➤ What is the essence of the gospel according to the verses you just read?

➤ What is the relationship between the message of the gospel, its recipient, and its deliverer?

➤ What should be our attitude regarding the personalities involved in gospel presentations?

➤ Evangelism is for every believer. What are some ways other than preaching that we can evangelize?

FRIENDSHIP, DISCIPLESHIP, AND EVANGELISM

Friendship and Evangelism

The concept of lifestyle, relational, or friendship evangelism acknowledges the oft-overlooked cultivation process in evangelism. Consider the aspects of friendship and evangelism in table 26.

MERGING FRIENDSHIP AND EVANGELISM

Friendship	Evangelism
Love	Truth
Actions	Reasons
Walk	Talk
Incarnation	Proclamation
Intention	Information

Table 26

➤ What shortcomings result if we pursue evangelism without friendship?

➤ What shortcomings result if we pursue friendship without evangelism?

We can be tempted to evangelize only when we think conversion in the moment is likely. However, this was not how Jesus approached ministry.

➤ What does the self-description of Jesus found in Matthew 11:19 tell us about how we should approach evangelism?·

> The Son of Man came eating and drinking, and they say, "Behold, a gluttonous man and a drunkard, a friend of tax collectors and sinners!" Yet wisdom is vindicated by her deeds.
>
> Matthew 11:19

Discipleship and Evangelism

Spiritual obstetrics should naturally and smoothly transition into spiritual pediatrics. This follow-up process requires love, patience, and acceptance, since growth is gradual and young children tend to make messes.

Conformed to His Image, Revised Edition, 418

The Great Commission (Matthew 28:18–20) calls for disciples, not merely decisions. When evangelism is accompanied by friendship and discipleship, the resulting relationships enrich our lives in the most meaningful of ways.

➢ Consider the words of Paul to the Thessalonians in the following quote. What elements of friendship, evangelism, and discipleship do you see exhibited in this passage?

You recall, brethren, our labor and hardship, how working night and day so as not to be a burden to any of you, we proclaimed to you the gospel of God. You are witnesses, and so is God, how devoutly and uprightly and blamelessly we behaved toward you believers; just as you know how we were exhorting and encouraging and imploring each one of you as a father would his own children, so that you would walk in a manner worthy of the God who calls you into His own kingdom and glory.

For this reason we also constantly thank God that when you received the word of God which you heard from us, you accepted it not as the word of men, but for what it really is, the word of God, which also performs its work in you who believe.

1 Thessalonians 2:9–13

Nurturing Spirituality

OVERCOMING THE BARRIERS TO EVANGELISM

KEY VERSES

He said to His disciples, "The harvest is plentiful, but the workers are few. Therefore beseech the Lord of the harvest to send out workers into His harvest."

Matthew 9:37–38

SUGGESTED READING

Conformed to His Image, Revised Edition, chapter 33

BARRIERS FOR BELIEVERS

Fear is perhaps the primary barrier to evangelism. And perhaps the primary passage regarding fear is Paul's instruction to Timothy:

God has not given us a spirit of timidity, but of power and love and discipline. Therefore do not be ashamed of the testimony of our Lord or of me His prisoner, but join with me in suffering for the gospel according to the power of God.

2 Timothy 1:7–8

➤ How can each of the following help you overcome the barrier of fear?

• Power

• Love

• Discipline

Paul also charges Timothy to do the work of an evangelist. A look at the context of this command may help us understand why Paul emphasized the need for power, love, and discipline from the Lord.

> I solemnly charge you in the presence of God and of Christ Jesus, who is to judge the living and the dead, and by His appearing and His kingdom: preach the word; be ready in season and out of season; reprove, rebuke, exhort, with great patience and instruction. For the time will come when they will not endure sound doctrine; but wanting to have their ears tickled, they will accumulate for themselves teachers in accordance to their own desires, and will turn away their ears from the truth and will turn aside to myths. But you, be sober in all things, endure hardship, *do the work of an evangelist*, fulfill your ministry.
>
> For I am already being poured out as a drink offering, and the time of my departure has come. I have fought the good fight, I have finished the course, I have kept the faith; in the future there is laid up for me the crown of righteousness, which the Lord, the righteous Judge, will award to me on that day; and not only to me, but also to all who have loved His appearing.
>
> 2 Timothy 4:1–8, emphasis added

➤ How would you characterize the context in which Timothy was to preach the gospel?

➤ It appears that in the case of some listeners, failure was certain. How does this context shape your view of the duty of evangelism?

➤ What repeated inspiration is found in the opening and closing of this passage?

➤ This video session discussed the following barriers to evangelism: method, fear, inadequacy, indifference, time, and isolation. Which of these barriers do you identify most with, and why?

BARRIERS FOR UNBELIEVERS

Unbelievers face three types of barriers when others try to evangelize them: emotional, intellectual, and volitional. Emotional barriers include negative attitudes and associations (often due to past experiences or relational tensions), intellectual barriers involve misconceptions of or objections to the truth claims of Christianity, and the volitional barrier relates to a person's sinful nature that is at enmity with God (a barrier overcome only by the ministry of the Holy Spirit).

➤ When it comes to evangelizing others, which of these three barriers most concerns you?

➤ How can your understanding of evangelism as a process help to overcome an unbeliever's emotional barriers?

Consider yet another charge to Timothy:

Refuse foolish and ignorant speculations, knowing that they produce quarrels. The Lord's bond-servant must not be quarrelsome, but be kind to all, able to teach, patient when wronged, with gentleness correcting those who are in opposition, if perhaps God may grant them repentance leading to the knowledge of the truth, and they may come to their senses and escape from the snare of the devil, having been held captive by him to do his will.

2 Timothy 2:23-26

➤ What principles are given here for refuting intellectual opposition to the gospel?

➤ Where in this passage do you see the volitional barrier to evangelism?

The modern apologetics movement in this age of information gives believers (and unbelievers) great resources for answering intellectual objections to the gospel. These resources—blogs, podcasts, websites, books—serve both as tools with which you can train and as points of discussion you can use to begin the process of relational evangelism. Some suggestions for apologetics training include:

- Read (or reread) *The Case for Faith* or *The Case for Christ* by journalist and atheist-turned-Christian Lee Strobel.
- Explore *kenboa.org/apologetics*, where you can read articles, watch discussions, or explore our summary of the evidence of God's existence, called *20 Compelling Evidences That God Exists* (direct link: *kenboa.org/apologetics/20-compelling-evidences-that-god-exists*).

- Check out Summit Ministries' online resources and conferences for both young people and adults: *www.summit.org*.
- Train yourself to anticipate and answer. Keep a list of difficult questions and your answers to them. Review this list so that you can be prepared when people ask.
- Pick an apologetics topic or resource that appeals to you and start a discussion group. The group might consist of believers who want to strengthen their faith or of believers and unbelievers interested in exploring the claims.

THE CONTEXT OF EVANGELISM

Lessons from History

Paul found himself in difficult places to evangelize, such as Athens, Greece. The way he acted in this situation can teach you principles for how to approach evangelistic ministry in your life. Read Acts 17:16–34 and then answer the following questions.

➤ How did the cultural context affect Paul?

➤ With whom was Paul sharing the gospel?

➤ In what venues did he share the gospel?

➤ With what frequency did Paul share the gospel?

➤ In the face of which intellectual barriers did Paul share the gospel?

➤ In the face of which emotional barriers did Paul share the gospel?

➤ In verses 26–27, how does Paul speak to the barriers of fear, inadequacy, isolation, and volition?

➤ What do the different reactions of those in the crowd teach you about evangelism?

Prayer and Action

Consider Paul's instructions to the Colossians for interacting with unbelievers.

Conduct yourselves with wisdom toward outsiders, making the most of the opportunity. Let your speech always be with grace, as though seasoned with salt, so that you will know how you should respond to each person.

Colossians 4:5–6

PRAY: Pray for God's empowerment in your words and work as well as in your walk and talk as you encounter those who don't yet share in the joy of abundant life that you possess.

Consider the following spheres of evangelism. Pray over each network, and ask God to give you the opportunity, confidence, and graciousness needed to share the gospel with them through both your words and your actions.

- Family

- Friends

- Coworkers

- Neighbors

Corporate Spirituality

THE NEED FOR COMMUNITY

KEY VERSE

The grace of the Lord Jesus Christ, and the love of God, and the fellowship of the Holy Spirit, be with you all.

2 Corinthians 13:14

SUGGESTED READING

Conformed to His Image, Revised Edition, chapter 34

COMMUNITY IN A DIGITAL AGE

You as an individual are to conform to the image of Christ, but you are also called to grow in community as part of the body of Christ. From the creation of the church, believers were identified by their strong communal bond. Yet believers in this present age experience the possibility for community in a way that was unavailable to prior generations. The phenomenon of social media has created a paradoxical situation in which we can readily make connections in isolation.

➤ What challenges does social media present to community?

➤ What advantages does social media create for community?

➤ How does the time people spend engaging in digital community affect community living as a whole?

➤ What challenges to self-identity does social media present for the individual?

➤ Media can both reflect and shape community. How does our tendency to promote false images of our lives (impression management) shape the way we view others and ourselves?

➤ Has social media caused you to think more of yourself or of others?

Our call to be cautious is not a Luddite or reactionary approach (this study guide, after all, pairs with digital media!). Rather it is a call to understand the times, with their opportunities and challenges. Consider the following quote.

> *We cannot return to the past, but we can learn how to treasure relationships as ends rather than means, and we can recapture a transcending biblical vision of commitment and community that will make us more human and less controlled by our culture.*
>
> *Conformed to His Image, Revised Edition, 440*

THE INDIVIDUAL IN COMMUNITY

A wise approach to community living appropriates truths from across the spectrum and is aware of the dangers of living at one extreme while eschewing the other. Extreme views regarding community include isolationism and institutionalism. Isolationism minimizes the value of community, whereas institutionalism minimizes the value of the individual.

➤ What is lost if we live in the extreme of isolationism?

➤ What is lost if we live in the extreme of institutionalism?

As with all facets of spirituality, our goal is conformity with Jesus. His life is our example of the individual in community. Trace the actions and interactions of Jesus through Matthew 14:13–36.

➤ What mixes of isolation and community do you observe?

➤ What patterns of interaction emerge?

➤ What impels the shifts from interaction to solitude and from solitude to interaction?

Matthew gives another glimpse into the life of Jesus later in his gospel. Here, too, you'll find an example from Jesus of living in community. Now with Matthew 26:36–46, observe the interactions of Jesus and answer the same questions of this text.

➤ What mixes of isolation and community do you observe?

➤ What patterns of interaction emerge?

➤ What impels the shifts from interaction to solitude and from solitude to interaction?

➤ Consider the two passages from Matthew (14:13–36 and 26:36–46) that you just examined. How do these separate but similar glimpses into the life of Jesus help you understand life in solitude, community, and ministry?

UNITY, DIVERSITY, AND COMMUNITY IN THE TRINITY

The fellowship of the Trinity is the foundation for our communal life. We are invited to unite as individuals and communities in this fellowship with one another and with God, as John explains in his first epistle:

What was from the beginning, what we have heard, what we have seen with our eyes, what we have looked at and touched with our hands, concerning the Word of Life—and the life was manifested, and we have seen and testify and proclaim to you the eternal life, which was with the Father and was manifested to us—what we have seen and heard we proclaim to you also, so that you too may have fellowship with us; and indeed our fellowship is with the Father, and with His Son Jesus Christ. These things we write, so that our joy may be made complete.

1 John 1:1-4

➤ What is the result of entering into this fellowship that John describes? How does this result shape your view of the purpose of community? Of evangelism?

➤ Notice the pattern of fellowship that emerges, and mark the instances in 1 John 1:1–4 where you see:

- Fellowship of the Father with the Son
- Fellowship of the Son with the apostles
- Fellowship of the apostles with other disciples

➤ Note that this same pattern can be observed in John 15:9–12. Mark the three examples of fellowship again, as you did with 1 John 1:1–4.

Just as the Father has loved Me, I have also loved you; abide in My love. If you keep My commandments, you will abide in My love; just as I have kept My Father's commandments and abide in His love. These things I have spoken to you so that My joy may be in you, and that your joy may be made full.
    This is My commandment, that you love one another, just as I have loved you.

John 15:9-12

➤ What purpose or result do you notice repeated in this passage of John?

➤ Christ's prayer to the Father in John 17:13–26 speaks, once again, of the relationships between the Father and the Son, the Son and the apostles, and the apostles and the world. Carefully read this passage and trace the lines of relationship that emerge there. Notice too the stated purpose in verse 13. What do the repetitions of this pattern and the result of fellowship signify about the importance of Christian fellowship?

CHALLENGES TO COMMUNITY

We were created for fellowship—both with God and with each other. But sin's entrance into the world radically affected our ability to flourish in community.

➤ Read Genesis 3. What levels of alienation do you observe?

➤ Much of the New Testament's writing was occasioned by problems in community. Identify the problems of community found in the following passages. As you study, consider how you can be a source of joy to your community and not a source of strife.

- Acts 6:1–4

- 1 Corinthians 1:10–17

- 1 Corinthians 4:18–5:2

- Galatians 1:6–7

- 1 Timothy 6:3–6

- James 4:1–6

- 3 John 9–11

PRAY: This last facet, corporate spirituality, is a fitting bookend to the first facet, relational spirituality, as both center on relationships. Pray with the following focuses:

- That you as an individual would love the Lord with all your being
- That your relationship with God would result in an overflow of love toward others
- That your identity in Christ would inform your identity in community
- That your service to the community would be a source of joy to others and a source of joy in your soul

Hell is self-centered and isolational; heaven is others-centered and relational. Corporate spirituality carries a high price because it requires us to go against the grain of our fallen instinct for privatization and control. But Scripture teaches us that it is more than worth the cost, since the greatest experiences of joy take place when they are shared with others. Joy quickly atrophies when it is hoarded. The spiritual life is not simply a matter between an individual and God; it was never meant to be privatized or individualistic but to be shared in community with the people of God. Our personal relationship with Jesus Christ is revealed and expressed in the ways we relate to the people around us.

Conformed to His Image, Revised Edition, 446

Corporate Spirituality

THE NATURE AND PURPOSE OF THE CHURCH

KEY VERSES

Speaking the truth in love, we are to grow up in all aspects into Him who is the head, even Christ, from whom the whole body, being fitted and held together by what every joint supplies, according to the proper working of each individual part, causes the growth of the body for the building up of itself in love.

Ephesians 4:15–16

SUGGESTED READING

Conformed to His Image, Revised Edition, chapter 35

THE NATURE OF THE CHURCH

➤ In the following passages, how is the church described?

- 1 Corinthians 3:16–17 _____
- 1 Corinthians 12:27 _____
- Ephesians 2:19–22 _____

- Ephesians 5:31–32   _____
- 1 Peter 2:9–10   _____

➤ With these descriptions in mind, identify the functions within the church that you observe in the following passages.

- Acts 2:42

- Romans 12

- 1 Corinthians 11:17–34

- 1 Corinthians 12

- 1 Corinthians 14

- Ephesians 4:11–16

- Ephesians 5:19–21

- Colossians 3:16

- Hebrews 10:23–25

➤ How well does your view of and practice within your own local church align with the descriptions and functions you see within Scripture?

DISTORTIONS OF THE BIBLICAL VISION

Just as individuals are targets of spiritual warfare, so too the church as a body consisting of those individuals is prone to attack. Consider how the church has been attacked, resulting in the following distortions of the body:

1. Abuse of the community for the purposes of power, control, or wealth
2. Identification as an institution consisting of buildings more than a living organism composed of people
3. The formation of identity cults with an unhealthy focus on lead pastors
4. A compromising of the milk and meat of God's Word with post-Enlightenment liberalism, postmodernism, or other cultural agendas
5. The growth of suburbia and proliferation of transportation options, resulting in the priority of subjective church experience
6. An uncritical use of models and techniques (business, psychology, entertainment) that manipulate rather than minister

➤ Which distortions have you witnessed in your church involvement?

➤ It's easy to find things we simply don't like because of taste and tradition. Are the distortions you just listed true distortions or merely acceptable alternatives to your preferences?

PRAY: As you consider problems within the church, know that it's easier to critique than encourage. Pray for your church, specifically for:

- Your pastor—encouragement, wisdom, peace at home, courage, rest, staff, relationships, joy, protection
- Your role—to encourage, evangelize, serve, worship, edify
- Your church's community—opportunities to serve, the spread of the gospel, local government leaders

➤ Examples of church distortions can be found in the opening chapters of Revelation. What issues do you observe as you read the risen Christ's message to the churches in Revelation 2–3?

PURPOSES OF THE CHURCH

Consider the list of corporate purposes presented in this video session. Examine the Scriptures associated with each of the following purposes, and then pray for that purpose of the church. Ask God how you can contribute to each purpose within the body of Christ.

1. Love and Compassion
   - Galatians 5:13–15
   - Colossians 3:12–14

   My prayer focus:

2. Identity and Purpose
   - Galatians 3:26–29
   - Philippians 2:1–2

   My prayer focus:

3. Nurture and Service
   - Ephesians 4:11–16
   - Philippians 2:3–4

   My prayer focus:

4. Discernment
   - 1 John 4:1–6
   - 1 Thessalonians 5:21

   My prayer focus:

5. Forgiveness and Reconciliation
   - 2 Corinthians 2:6–11
   - Ephesians 4:32

   My prayer focus:

6. Authority and Submission
   - Acts 20:28
   - Hebrews 13:17

My prayer focus:

7. Worship and Prayer
    ◦ Ephesians 5:19–20
    ◦ Colossians 3:16

My prayer focus:

Corporate Spirituality

SOUL CARE, LEADERSHIP, ACCOUNTABILITY, AND RENEWAL

KEY VERSE

A wise man will hear and increase in learning,

And a man of understanding will acquire wise counsel.

Proverbs 1:5

SUGGESTED READING

Conformed to His Image, Revised Edition, chapter 36

ALONG THE JOURNEY

Recall in the process spirituality sessions (22–24) our assertion that the best metaphor for life as a whole and for the spiritual life in particular is that of a journey. Using that metaphor, we'd be wise to understand that there are those who are farther along on the journey, those from whom we can gain insight and guidance.

The following verses in Proverbs address wise counsel. Use these verses to answer the following questions about character qualities needed for those on both the giving and receiving ends of spiritual guidance and direction.

- Proverbs 1:5
- Proverbs 9:9
- Proverbs 12:15
- Proverbs 19:20
- Proverbs 27:17

➤ What character qualities are needed for those who provide spiritual guidance and direction?

➤ What character qualities are needed in order to listen to spiritual guidance and direction?

Consider the suggestion, offered in this video session, that everyone should establish relationships in their lives akin to a Paul (the mentor farther along on the journey), a Barnabas (a peer on the journey), and a Timothy (someone to whom you can impart your experienced wisdom).

If you don't have people in your life who fulfill these roles, ask God to send such people into your life.

➤ Are there character issues you need to address before you can be a mentor to someone? A good start would be to share these issues with a Barnabas or Paul in your life.

➤ What will be missing from your life without these relationships?

SOUL CARE

The soul care ministries covered in this video session move from informal, unstructured, and reciprocal relationships to more formal, structured, unidirectional ones. While they may not always have been recognized by these titles, they are ministries which have always existed among the people of God.

Spiritual Friendship

➤ What character qualities are needed for the existence of this type of relationship?

➤ What circumstances are needed for this type of relationship to exist?

➤ If you are married, can you characterize your relationship with your spouse as a spiritual friendship? If you can't, focus on *your* shortcomings and identify your spouse's endearing qualities. If you're not praying together, start there.

Spiritual Guidance

What this category of relationships may lack in intimacy, it offers in wisdom and maturity. Perhaps you know of someone who has a spiritual maturity that you admire, even if you don't know the person well.

Think of someone in your church or someone involved in Christian ministry. Ask that person as many of the following questions as possible, either over lunch or via correspondence. (Fill in the blanks with the specifics of your situation.)

• What words of encouragement would you offer for my current stage of life?

- I'm considering _____. Do you have any experience or words of wisdom or warning in this area?

- I'm facing a decision (or dilemma). What actionable steps can you recommend for addressing the situation?

- I'm interested in (or debating) _____. Could you recommend any reading on the topic?

➤ Take notes on your exchange and consider whether this person might become a mentor. (See the following section.)

Spiritual Mentoring

The mentoring relationship has an increased level of involvement in the life of the mentee, though it may come in various forms or degrees. These are the markers of effective mentoring:

- Compatibility
- Clear purpose
- Regularity
- Accountability
- Open communication
- Confidentiality
- Definite life cycle (planned, particular stages from beginning to end of the mentoring relationship)
- Periodic evaluation
- Revision of expectations
- Closure (thoughtful consideration of how the mentoring relationship ends or achieves its goal)

If you're considering being a mentor, use the markers just listed to guide you.

➢ Which of these areas might you struggle with as a mentor? Are you willing to commit to those areas anyway?

➢ If you're already in a mentoring role, which, if any, of these markers is missing? What can you do to address this shortcoming to the relationship?

Spiritual Direction

Spiritual directors help people discern the workings of grace in their lives and offer guidance and clarity for one's spiritual direction. This ancient practice has been seldom noticed by Protestants until recent times.

Read the following quote, making note of the character qualities that must be present in a spiritual director. Then answer the question that follows.

> *[Spiritual] directors must be sought out, but it is not easy to find them. When we do, we should not expect them to flatter us or cater to our illusions. Instead, we must approach them in a spirit of humility and let them know what we think, feel, and desire. Good directors will ask appropriate questions, listen skillfully, reveal barriers to growth, assist in confession and repentance, show how to listen to God and how to implement spiritual disciplines, rebuke and encourage as necessary, and offer their presence and compassion. Spiritual directors have skill in distinguishing between spiritual and psychological problems (e.g., spiritual aridity versus psychosomatic illness or infantile moodiness).*
>
> *Conformed to His Image, Revised Edition, 467*

➢ Which qualities or activities would be helpful for you in your current journey?

PRAY: Ask God to supply the hope, affirmation, and honest yet gentle engagement from a spiritual director or other soul friend.

SERVANT LEADERSHIP, ACCOUNTABILITY, AND RENEWAL

Servant Leadership

God has appointed certain people for shepherding and leadership in churches and ministries. These leaders are called to emulate Christ's example of serving rather than seeking to be served (Mark 10:45).

➤ Hebrews 13:7 says, "Remember those who led you, who spoke the word of God to you; and considering the result of their conduct, imitate their faith." What elements of servant leadership do you observe in this verse?

Those called to servant leadership should understand the temptations that prevent one from fulfilling that calling. Consider the temptations listed here (from Henri Nouwen's *In the Name of Jesus*).

- The temptation of relevancy
- The temptation to be spectacular (acquiring plaudits and popularity)
- The temptation to be powerful

➤ Which of the twelve facets of spirituality will help you resist the temptation of relevancy, by loving Jesus more than your accomplishments?

➤ Which facet will help you resist the temptation to be spectacular or popular, by immersing yourself in a confessing and caring community?

➢ Which facet will help you resist the temptation to be powerful, by seeking surrender to the leadership of Jesus?

Accountability and Renewal

➢ What areas of accountability are covered by the following verses?

- Galatians 2:14

- Romans 14:15

- Hebrews 13:17

➢ In what unique way does each of the three verses that you just read teach you about the others-focused requirement of servant leadership?

➢ Accountability requires the discipline of submitting oneself to another authority. What core Christian principles must be agreed to by both parties if true and effective accountability is to take place?

At the heart of pure accountability is a love toward God and neighbor. Relational spirituality leads to corporate spirituality. Let the following passage guide your heart and mind as you renew your soul and strength.

> Let us not lose heart in doing good, for in due time we will reap if we do not grow weary. So then, while we have opportunity, let us do good to all people, and especially to those who are of the household of the faith.
>
> Galatians 6:9-10

➤ Just as relational spirituality leads to corporate spirituality, individual renewal leads to corporate renewal. What is significant about the pronouns used in Galatians 6:9–10?

PRAY: Prayerfully consider whether you could partner with a like-minded sojourner such that your collective commitment to devotion to Christ might bring about an internal, invisible renewal in each of your lives and spark an external, visible renewal in your community.

True renewal is not a matter of institutional reorganization or public appeal; rather, it centers on the power of the Spirit (fire), the authority of the Word (fuel), and unity in prayer (fellowship) within the remnant of committed believers in the body of Christ. When prayer becomes pervasive, when passion becomes contagious, and when the power of God becomes evident, the community of faith grows both in quality (discipleship) and in quantity (evangelism).

Conformed to His Image, Revised Edition, 475

Moving Forward

THE NEED FOR DIVERSITY

KEY VERSE

Be devoted to one another in brotherly love; give preference to one another in honor.

Romans 12:10

SUGGESTED READING

Conformed to His Image, Revised Edition, appendix A

TYPES OF CHRISTIAN SPIRITUALITY

➢ As you've gone through this study, no doubt some topics have appealed to you more than others. Consider the twelve facets we've covered. In the very first session, you noted facets you gravitated toward. Now that you have a better idea of what each facet entails, rank their appeal to you, from one to twelve, with one being most appealing and twelve being least appealing.

_____ Relational	_____ Motivated	_____ Spirit-filled
_____ Paradigm	_____ Devotional	_____ Warfare
_____ Disciplined	_____ Holistic	_____ Nurturing
_____ Exchanged life	_____ Process	_____ Corporate

This video session mentioned four types of Christian spirituality—*apophatic/mind*, *kataphatic/mind*, *apophatic/heart*, and *kataphatic/heart*—which are based on work by Urban T. Holmes in *A History of Christian Spirituality*. These are reflected in figure 9 on the next page.

> **KATAPHATIC:** from a Greek word meaning "affirmative," stresses the knowledge of God through general and special revelation

> **APOPHATIC:** from a Greek word meaning "negative," stresses God's transcendence and mystery

➤ Which of the four quadrants in figure 9 would you place yourself in, and where in that quadrant? Place an X there.

➤ How is each end of the two spectrums (apophatic-kataphatic and mind-heart) necessary for the body of Christ?

Now look at table 27, which draws a very general correlation between the facets and each of the four spirituality types.

CHRISTIAN SPIRITUALITY TYPES AND THE TWELVE FACETS OF SPIRITUALITY

Apophatic/Mind	Kataphatic/Mind
• Corporate spirituality • Holistic spirituality • Warfare spirituality	• Paradigm spirituality • Motivated spirituality • Nurturing spirituality
Apophatic/Heart	**Kataphatic/Heart**
• Devotional spirituality • Disciplined spirituality • Process spirituality	• Relational spirituality • Exchanged life spirituality • Spirit-filled spirituality

Table 27

➤ Do the facets listed under your type mirror (or come close to mirroring) the ones you ranked most highly?

TYPES OF CHRISTIAN SPIRITUALITY

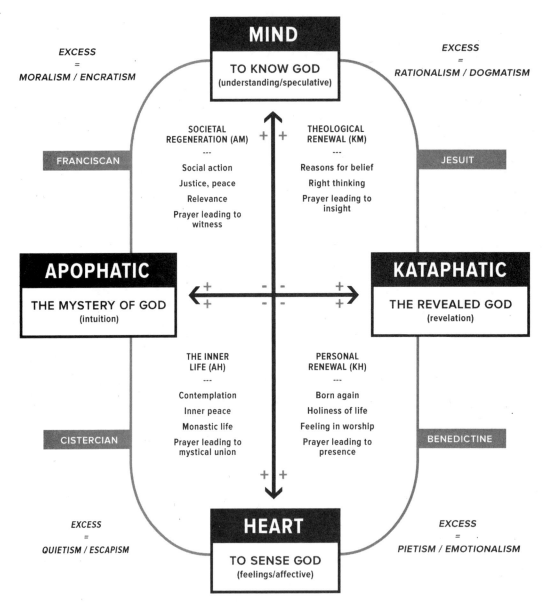

Figure 9

Based on "A Circle of Sensibility" from *A History of Christian Spirituality*
© 1980 by Urban Holmes III. Used by permission.

➤ Do the facets under the opposite of your type mirror (or come close to mirroring) the ones you ranked lowest?

➤ Are you willing to pursue one of the facets under your opposite type to bring greater diversity and balance in your spiritual life? If you are, how will you do so?

PERSONALITY TYPES, TEMPERAMENTS, AND THE FACETS

If you've taken a Myers-Briggs Type Indicator (MBTI) test, pull out your results now. If you haven't, take the test now at *mbtionline.com* (hint: you can find a free unofficial version of the test online if you prefer).

Your MBTI:

With your MBTI personality type in mind, consider table 28,[18] which describes the spiritual preferences and orientation of each of the sixteen possible types.

SPIRITUALITY AND PRAYER PRACTICE TENDENCIES FOR MYERS-BRIGGS PERSONALITY TYPES

ISTJ: Introverted Sensing with Thinking	**ISFJ: Introverted Sensing with Feeling**
• Serious, quiet, thorough, orderly, logical, private • Sense of responsibility • Private spirituality • Enjoys scheduled and consistent prayer • Conscience orientation; will of God	• Dependable, conservative, strong sense of duty, often taken for granted • Desires to please God • Attracted to orderly spiritual regimen • Silent, private prayer • Community orientation; present expression of spirituality
ISTP: Introverted Thinking with Sensing	**ISFP: Introverted Feeling with Sensing**
• Practical, precise, reserved, objective • Action over prayer; practice of the presence of God • Individual approach to prayer and spiritual growth • Needs time for private meditation • Thinking and concentration, but needs practical application	• Free spirit, impulsive, intense feelings • Artistic, appreciation for life • Open to social dimensions of personal spirituality • Flexible prayer forms; needs the discipline of private reflection • Present-tense, experiential orientation

Table 28

(cont.)

ESTP: Extroverted Sensing with Thinking	ESFP: Extroverted Sensing with Feeling
• Action-oriented; pragmatic, realistic; unpredictable and flexible • Experiences of community, praise, singing • Requires minimal spiritual structure • Spontaneous prayers • Communal theological orientation	• Charismatic, attractive personalities • Lives primarily for the moment • People-oriented spirituality • Attracted to religious externals • Generous servants, accepting of others • Community orientation
ESTJ: Extroverted Thinking with Sensing	**ESFJ: Extroverted Feeling with Sensing**
• Responsible, orderly, administrative skills, realistic, conservative • Organized approach to spiritual growth, consistent • Institutional spirituality • Practical theological orientation	• Highly sociable, friendly, sympathetic, sentimental, caring • Attracted to prayer groups • Intercessory prayers • Practical application of spirituality • Attracted to experiential mysticism
INFJ: Introverted Intuition with Feeling	**INTJ: Introverted Intuition with Thinking**
• Gentle, compassionate, accepting, inspirational; can be stubborn • Not attracted to formal or repetitive prayer • Need for silence; contemplative and conversational prayer • Spiritually reflective on daily events • Mystical orientation	• Self-confident, decisive, pragmatic, single-minded, independent • High achiever; controlling, determined; logically oriented • Attracted to new insights, ideas, inspirations, improvements • Introspective prayer life • Needs time for spiritual reflection
INFP: Introverted Feeling with Intuition	**INTP: Introverted Thinking with Intuition**
• Idealistic, subjective interpretation; noble service for the benefit of others • Solitary and silent prayer • Personal, spontaneous response to God • Spiritual reflection on daily activities • Desires human support of spiritual development	• Good memory, intelligent, power of concentration, problem solver • Prefers to pray alone; logical, coherent prayer form • Needs space for concentration and evaluation of spiritual insights • Attracted to theological concepts; appraiser of new spiritual insights
ENFP: Extroverted Intuition with Feeling	**ENTP: Extroverted Intuition with Thinking**
• Optimistic, enthusiastic, imaginative, highly intuitive, skilled with people • Needs significant time for prayerful reflection • Spontaneous, unstructured prayer • Not institutionally motivated • People-oriented spirituality; able to deal with different people and events	• Ingenious, open to new possibilities, resourceful, enthusiastic, innovative • Enjoys novelty, originality, and new forms of prayer • Spontaneous, improvised prayers • Not inclined to a spiritual regimen • Attracted to spiritual conversations with others

Table 28   *(cont.)*

ENFJ: Extroverted Feeling with Intuition	ENTJ: Extroverted Thinking with Intuition
• Motivates people, persuasive, natural leader • Comfortable with many types of prayer; needs time for reflection • Dislikes repetition and routine • People-centered spiritual orientation	• Effective leader, seeks power and competency, outgoing organizer • Theological spirituality • Need experiences of community • Attracted to structured, logical, consistent prayer forms

Table 28

➤ How do the descriptions under each personality type help expand your view and understanding of diversity within the body of Christ?

➤ Do the bullet points under your type seem accurate?

➤ Find out the MBTI of your spouse (or of someone else you live with or your closest friend if you're not married). Does this information give you some insight into why you may have either differing or similar approaches to your spiritual life?

There are four basic MBTI temperaments, defined in table 29:[19]

THE FOUR MYERS-BRIGGS TYPE INDICATOR TEMPERAMENTS

SJ Temperament: ESTJ, ISTJ, ESFJ, ISFJ	SP Temperament: ESFP, ISFP, ESTP, ISTP
NF Temperament: ENFJ, INFJ, ENFP, INFP	NT Temperament: ENTJ, INTJ, ENTP, INTP

Table 29

Your MBTI temperament:

Locate your MBTI temperament in table 30, which shows the spirituality facets to which each temperament generally correlates.

MYERS-BRIGGS TEMPERAMENTS AND THE TWELVE FACETS OF SPIRITUALITY

SJ Temperament	SP Temperament
• Disciplined spirituality • Motivated spirituality • Holistic spirituality	• Corporate spirituality • Spirit-filled spirituality • Warfare spirituality
NF Temperament	**NT Temperament**
• Relational spirituality • Devotional spirituality • Exchanged life spirituality	• Paradigm spirituality • Process spirituality • Nurturing spirituality

Table 30

➤ How do the facets under your temperament line up with your rankings at the beginning of this session?

➤ Ponder for a moment why these particular facets correlate with your temperament.

> *Even when we acknowledge that there are several legitimate and complementary approaches to growth in the spiritual life, there is a natural tendency to limit ourselves to the one that best fits our personality and to assume that if it works for us, it should work for others.*
>
> *Conformed to His Image, Revised Edition, 496*

THE VALUE OF DIVERSITY

Personality tests and exercises like the ones you just completed aren't intended to put you (or others) in a box or to excuse behavior; rather they can be tools for understanding yourself better and for understanding how others in the body of Christ can enrich your spiritual walk.

➤ How can these exercises be liberating?

➤ How are they helpful for warding off discouragement or unwarranted feelings of inadequacy?

➤ How might understanding different personalities and temperaments help you avoid conflict with other believers?

➤ Have you ever clashed with—or dismissed as "weird" or "less spiritual"—a fellow believer who you now realize may have simply had a different personality type or temperament?

➤ Read 1 Corinthians 12:4–26 and Romans 12:4–8. What role does diversity play in the body of Christ?

➤ Read 1 Corinthians 13:1–3 and Romans 12:9–13. Gifts may differ, but what is non-negotiable in the body of Christ?

The more you accept the need for this dynamic tension between affirming your natural dispositions and engaging in less preferred ways of being and doing, the more full-orbed and Christlike you will become in your spiritual journey. . . . All of us, regardless of temperament and natural aptitude, need a healthy balance of doctrine, experience, and practice.

Conformed to His Image, Revised Edition, 508

Looking Back

THE RICHNESS OF OUR HERITAGE

KEY VERSE

We are from God; he who knows God listens to us; he who is not from God does not listen to us. By this we know the spirit of truth and the spirit of error.

1 John 4:6

SUGGESTED READING

Conformed to His Image, Revised Edition, appendix B

BROADENING OUR PERSPECTIVE

Diversity in the body of Christ appears not only across the church today, in terms of individual temperament and personality differences, but also across the centuries of church history.

➤ This video session made the following observation: "There's a tendency to become so focused in our contemporary milieu that we forget that we're building on a whole collective of historical precedence that shapes and defines how we practice and think." How did you react when you heard this statement? Do you agree with it?

➤ Have you been too narrowly focused in the modern church context? If so, how?

➤ Assess your reading and exposure to teachers of the main different eras and traditions (listed in table 31). If your exposure is limited and your focus narrow, what might you gain by branching out? What dangers or risks are there?

THE MAJOR CHURCH ERAS AND TRADITIONS

Historic Diversity	Modern Church: Traditions (and Branches)
Ancient church (Pentecost to AD 600)	Catholicism
Medieval church (AD 600 to 1500)	Orthodoxy (Eastern and Western)
Modern church (AD 1500 to present)	Protestantism (Lutheran, Reformed, Anabaptist, Anglican)

Table 31

➤ Read 1 John 4:1–6 and Ephesians 1:17. How are we to assess various movements and figures in the history of the church?

➤ *The past informs the present.* Learning history helps us avoid being bound by our own parochial views. Do you have a desire to broaden your perspective and exposure? If so, in what ways?

If church history is of great interest to you, we recommend the following resources.

- *A History of Christian Spirituality* (Urban T. Holmes)
- *Thirsty for God: A Brief History of Christian Spirituality*, 3rd ed. (Bradley P. Holt)
- *Why You Think the Way You Do: The Story of Western Worldviews from Rome to Home* (Glenn S. Sunshine)

The combination of your nature (temperament) and nurture (culture) will predispose you to particular styles of spirituality, but as we argued before, it is helpful to stretch yourself through the discipline of deliberate exposure to a facet of spirituality you would ordinarily overlook or avoid.

Conformed to His Image, Revised Edition, 542

SPIRITUALITY IN THE ANCIENT AND MEDIEVAL CHURCH

Reflect on how the church grew in each period described below, noting God's faithfulness to his people through multiple generations and circumstances.

- The *ancient* church enjoyed rapid multiplication across Asia, Europe, and Africa in spite of persecution and even martyrdom. The date AD 313—when the Roman emperor Constantine declared Christianity legal in the Roman Empire—marks a watershed moment. After that, the church became more institutionalized, with growing political and financial power.
- The *medieval* church grew in power and prosperity, evidenced by great cathedrals and art. Additionally, the church supported the development of universities and scholarly work in law, theology, philosophy, and science. The pope became a secular ruler while making increasing claims to authority over the whole Christian world, leading to a split with the Orthodox church. Opposition to the church's wealth and power contributed to developments in monastic spirituality and reform orders such as the Franciscans.
- The *modern* period, sparked by the Protestant Reformation, has seen expansion of Christianity beyond Europe—to the Americas and, more recently, throughout the Global South—alongside renewed vitality and spiritual fervor.

In the later part of the ancient church, *mysticism* became an important theme in Christian spirituality. This is a good example of an ancient practice that is frequently misunderstood. It can have both biblical and unbiblical forms.

BIBLICAL MYSTICISM: personal apprehension of the transcendent God

UNBIBLICAL MYSTICISM: oneness (absorption and loss of identity in God, or oneness with created things or nature)

➤ When you hear the word mysticism, which of its two forms comes to mind—biblical or unbiblical? Why is that? Do you need to revise your understanding of this concept?

Reminder: Terminology evolves with time. A good question to ask when reading older Christian writings is, "What did they mean by that?" Keep this in mind as you do the next exercise.

EXERCISE: A significant number of "road maps" and insights were left by Christians across these three eras in the church. It's likely that you are already familiar with many modern figures. Therefore today (or this week, if you're out of time or doing this study in a group) explore at least one figure from each of the earlier eras of the church. Suggestions follow. Try to seek original sources and/or historical sources that strive to be objective.

Ancient Church
- *Top suggestion:* Augustine of Hippo (consider reading his *Confessions,* which is widely recognized as the first Western autobiography)
- Perpetua
- Justin Martyr
- Tertullian
- Origen of Alexandria
- Antony (or any of the other desert fathers)
- Benedict
- Basil of Caesarea

Medieval Church
- *Top suggestion:* Thomas à Kempis (consider reading his *The Imitation of Christ*)
- Anselm of Canterbury
- Bernard of Clairvaux
- Thomas Aquinas
- Francis of Assisi
- Catherine of Genoa
- Julian of Norwich

THE MODERN CHURCH AND BEYOND

It's impossible in so short a space to cover the full gamut of Christianity in the modern era (since the Protestant Reformation). Glenn Sunshine has a wonderful set of resources available at *www.esquareinch.com* on the Reformation and its ongoing legacy. We encourage you to explore some of his historical articles.

A Balanced Approach

> *Unbalanced extremes are always unbiblical, and they force an either-or on a number of areas that are better viewed as both-and.*
>
> *Conformed to His Image, Revised Edition,* 534

➤ Review the themes in table 32 that can be observed throughout the history of the church. History has seen a number of pendulum swings related to these issues. Where would you fall on these continuums in terms of your *emphasis* in each area? (Place an X at that spot for each continuum.) The ideal is a balanced affirmation of both ends (i.e., an X in the middle).

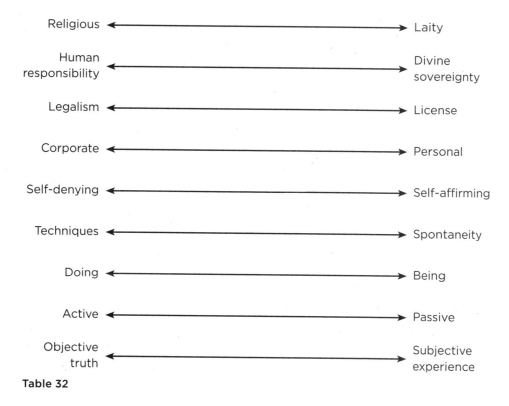

Religious	⟷	Laity
Human responsibility	⟷	Divine sovereignty
Legalism	⟷	License
Corporate	⟷	Personal
Self-denying	⟷	Self-affirming
Techniques	⟷	Spontaneity
Doing	⟷	Being
Active	⟷	Passive
Objective truth	⟷	Subjective experience

Table 32

> *Many writers through the centuries have distinguished three approaches to Christian living: the active life, the contemplative life, and the mixed life. The first focuses on doing more than being, the second focuses on being more than doing, and the third approach, which I recommend, is a balanced combination of being and doing in which the latter flows out of the former.*
>
> *Conformed to His Image, Revised Edition, 542*

➤ After reading this quote, would you characterize yourself as one who lives an active life, a contemplative life, or a mixed life (balancing the two)?

Jesus himself struck the perfect balance; he was the ideal contemplative in action, taking the solitude of God with him everywhere he went, whether in a boat with the disciples, alone on the Mount of Olives, or in a crowd.

Kenneth Boa, *Life in the Presence of God*

Conclusion

CONTINUING ON THE JOURNEY: WHAT IT TAKES TO FINISH WELL

KEY VERSE

I have fought the good fight, I have finished the course, I have kept the faith.

2 Timothy 4:7

SUGGESTED READING

Conformed to His Image, Revised Edition, conclusion

JOURNEYING WELL: KEYS OF BEING

➤ Assessing your spiritual journey, would you characterize your most recent years as ones of steadily pursuing Jesus or years of increasing indifference—or something in between?

Now that you've almost completed this study guide, our prayer is that you're moved to either continue to journey well or start journeying well. Let these verses be an inspiration.

For this reason it says,

"Awake, sleeper,
And arise from the dead,
and Christ will shine on you."

Therefore be careful how you walk, not as unwise men but as wise, making the most of your time, because the days are evil.

Ephesians 5:14–16

Wake up, and strengthen the things that remain, which were about to die; for I have not found your deeds completed in the sight of My God.

Revelation 3:2

Intimacy with Christ

Your conformity to Christ in this life is contingent upon the closeness of your relationship with him. (We become like the company we keep.) Knowing Christ is also the key to any success, happiness, joy, and flourishing we enjoy along the journey.

➤ What is the effect on the following aspects of journeying well if you fail to seek intimacy with Jesus?

- Being faithful in spiritual disciplines

- Having a biblical perspective on the circumstances of life

- Having a teachable, responsive, humble, obedient spirit

- Having a clear sense of purpose and calling

- Having healthy relationship with others

- Making ongoing ministry investment in the lives of others

➢ How is it possible to have intimacy with someone you've never seen? Use the following verses to guide your answer: John 20:29; 1 Peter 1:7; 1 John 1:1–3; 3:2–3.

➢ Excessive love of things in the following categories can threaten your intimacy with Christ. For each category, list a possible threat in your life. Pray and guard against this threat. Talk to a friend, mentor, guide, and/or pastor about this list.

- People

- Possessions (or pursuit of them)

- Position (rank or role)

➤ Which do you want to be known for—loving Jesus or avoiding sin? Pray that desire for him would be your unrivaled passion.

Fidelity in Spiritual Disciplines

Our greatest tools in pursuing a lifetime of intimacy with Christ are spiritual disciplines. A disciplined life will not come without patience and responsiveness. Consider this description of the journey:

> *In each case we will choose to walk by sight or by faith, by law or by grace, by the flesh or by the Spirit, by our will or God's will, by submission or resistance, by dependence or by autonomy, by worldly wisdom or by divine wisdom, by betting everything on God's promises and character or by trying to control our world on our own terms, by the temporal or by the eternal, by trying to find our lives or by losing them for Christ's sake. Until we see Christ, we will always be engaged in this warfare in which we are tempted on a daily basis to drop out of the process of the obedience of faith.*
>
> *Conformed to His Image, Revised Edition, 487–88*

EXERCISE: It would be wise to schedule regular assessments that take into account your actions, attitudes, habits, and growth. Schedule this type of assessment in your calendar. Also, schedule review sessions with friends, mentors, pastors, and/or your spouse, as appropriate. (Remember that these disciplines are not ends in themselves. Our purpose in using them should always be to grow in intimacy with Jesus.)

JOURNEYING WELL: KEYS OF KNOWING

A Biblical Perspective on the Circumstances of Life

As we age, there comes a point of diminishing capacity and increasing responsibility. Trace the process exhibited in Romans 5:3–5.

➤ How will each of the following aspects help you maintain perspective as you journey onward?

- Perseverance through trial

- Proven character

- Hope

- Filled heart

Difficulties of life can drive us to futile despair or pleasure-seeking in this life, or difficulties can inspire us to invest all that we have in the next life. If you choose to invest everything you are and have into the life to come, you will gain the skills for traveling.

➤ These skills are present in the following verses. Read these verses now, and write down the traveling skill(s) you see in each.

- Matthew 6:25–34

- Philippians 4:11–13

- Hebrews 6:13–20

A Teachable, Responsive, Humble, Obedient Spirit

➢ Of the four adjectives in this key of knowing (teachable, responsive, humble, obedient), which do you find hardest? Easiest?

Meditate on Psalm 92:12–15.

> The righteous man will flourish like the palm tree,
> He will grow like a cedar in Lebanon.
> Planted in the house of the LORD,
> They will flourish in the courts of our God.
> They will still yield fruit in old age;
> They shall be full of sap and very green,
> To declare that the LORD is upright;
> He is my rock, and there is no unrighteousness in Him.
>
> Psalm 92:12–15

➢ List the privileges of the righteous, according to this passage.

➢ In this passage, what do you observe about the presence of the Lord?

➢ What do you observe about righteousness?

➤ Based on these observations, what can you say about the will of God for your life, especially as you grow older?

A Clear Sense of Personal Purpose and Calling

➤ Does the prospect of developing a clear sense of purpose and calling inspire you or cause panic?

Do not be tempted to pursue knowing your calling and purpose more than pursuing knowing Jesus.

> *We are first called to a Person, and then we are called to express this defining relationship in the things we undertake, realizing that the final outcome of our lives is in the hands of God. We have a sense of destiny, but our ignorance of the invisible geography of the new creation means that we must trust God for what he is calling us to become.*
>
> *Conformed to His Image, Revised Edition, 482-83*

Trusting God on your journey means trusting him not only with your eternal destiny but also with the final outcome of your life on earth—the sum of your life's service and pursuit. The outcome and total effect will always be invisible to you on this journey.

➤ How can this realization become an advantage for you in your journey?

PRAY: Ask God to clarify your personal vision of your purpose. Give this prayer some time; don't rush. Let it be guided by immersion in the Word.

JOURNEYING WELL: KEYS OF DOING

Healthy Relationships with Resourceful People

➤ With whom do you have healthy and resourceful relationships?

➤ What dangers result from not having healthy relationships with resourceful people in your journey?

➤ If this resource is lacking in your life, what personal shortcoming may be preventing you from seeking, or being sought out by, others? (Hint: It may have to do with a teachable, responsive, humble, and obedient spirit.)

Ongoing Ministry Investment in the Lives of Others

To have journeyed alone is to have failed. Consider Paul's declaration to the Thessalonians:

> Who is our hope or joy or crown of exultation? Is it not even you, in the presence of our Lord Jesus at His coming?
>
> 1 Thessalonians 2:19

People are not our projects or trophies; our growing intimacy with Christ should cause us to seek others to join in this fellowship.

> If there is any encouragement in Christ, if there is any consolation of love, if there is any fellowship of the Spirit, if any affection and compassion, make my joy complete by being of the same mind, maintaining the same love, united in spirit, intent on one purpose. Do nothing from selfishness or empty conceit, but with humility of mind regard one another as more important than yourselves.
>
> Philippians 2:1–3

➤ Consider whether someone you know, or even a small group of people, would benefit from going through this study. If so, we ask you to share it with them and even consider leading them through it.

PRAY: Prayerfully reflect on this study, on what you've learned, and on where you need to head from here in your spiritual life.

ACKNOWLEDGEMENTS

We would like to thank Matthew and Katie Robinson for their careful attention in editing this guide. They did so with an eye for excellence and a heart for those who would be walking through the Scriptures and the ideas presented. Additionally, their work in reviewing the accompanying video study resulted in a much better final resource. Those videos were also carefully reviewed by Angie Synan, a skilled videographer whose production insights were invaluable to us in our review. We're grateful also to Dr. Glenn Sunshine for his assistance in summarizing part of our session on church history. We recommend his resources at *https://esquareinch.com*. Finally, thank you to Katherine Kesey for refreshing the design of the figures in this guide. Her quick turnaround and patience with our tweaks enhanced and encouraged our work.

NOTES

1. Our app *Presence: Walk with God* makes these kinds of practices available at your fingertips (on your smartphone or computer). Visit *www.presence.app* for more info and to sign up for a fourteen-day free trial period. We'll provide you with example exercises later in this study guide. These exercises are also available in the book *A Guide to Practicing God's Presence* (available at *kenboa.org/shop*).

2. This is not a comprehensive list; there are other disciplines we could add. These twenty are based on both the example of Scripture (especially the practices of Jesus himself) and lists compiled by authors such as Richard Foster and Dallas Willard. Material is adapted from Ken Boa, *Conformed to His Image, Revised Edition*, 88–92.

3. We highly recommend the booklet *Perspectives on Prayer* (available at *kenboa.org/shop*) for tips on what, why, and how to pray. You can also download an electronic version free at *kenboa.org/perspectives-on-prayer*.

4. From Ken Boa, *Conformed to His Image, Revised Edition*, 108. This quote is from a seminary course Boa took from Hendricks.

5. This and the next exercises are from *www.presence.app*.

6. Answers to this exercise are: (1) Pursuing rewards is a biblical motivation. (2) Heaven isn't a reward; it's a gift, and gifts are freely given while rewards are earned through work. (3) Fear of loss and hope of reward are legitimate motivators.

7. Explore more exercises at *www.presence.app*.

8. For your own copy of these prayer cards, search for "Spiritual Renewal Collection" at *kenboa.org/shop*.

9. Explore more exercises at *www.presence.app*.

10. This guide is adapted from *A Journal of Sacred Readings: Spiritual Formation through Personal Encounters with Scripture*, available at *kenboa.org/shop*.

11. To give Christ priority, centrality.

12. Ordinary or insignificant.

13. From *www.presence.app*.

14. From *www.presence.app*.

15. For more on practicing God's presence, please refer to Kenneth Boa, *Life in the Presence of God: Practices for Living in Light of Eternity* (InterVarsity Press, 2017) as well as the companion training guide *A Guide to Practicing God's Presence* (Trinity House, 2018); the latter book serves as the basis for the app *Presence: Walk with God* (more info at *www.presence.app*).

16. This card is part of the "Spiritual Renewal Card Set," available at *kenboa.org/shop*.

17. This card is part of our "Spiritual Renewal Card Set," available at *kenboa.org/shop*.

18. This table distills work from various sources, principally Charles J. Keating, *Who We Are Is How We Pray*.

19. The creation of these four temperaments comes from the books *Type Talk* (by Otto Kroeger and Janet M. Thuesen) and *Please Understand Me* (by David Kiersey and Marilyn Bates).